contents

HEL

INTERWEAVE.
favorites

25 KNITTED ACCESSORIES
to *wear* and *share*

editors: **Allison Korleski with Erica Smith**

associate art director: **Julia Boyles**

cover and interior design: **Karla Baker**

photographer: **Joe Hancock** *except where noted*

production: **Katherine Jackson**

746.432

Interweave
A division of F+W Media, Inc.
4868 Innovation Drive
Fort Collins, CO 80525
interweave.com

Manufactured in China by RR Donnelley
Shenzhen

Library of Congress Cataloging-In-
Publication Data not available at time of
printing.

ISBN 978-1-62033-826-1 (pbk)
ISBN 978-1-62033-824-7 (PDF)

10 9 8 7 6 5 4 3 2 1

Additional Photo Credits

Carol Kaplan: Modern Quilt Wrap (page 24), Ene's Scarf
(page 102), and Lily of the Valley Shawl (page 108). Heather
Weston: Opera House Mitts (page 50) and Grand Army
Plaza Shawl (page 94). Rain Griffin Blond: Jasmin headscarf
(page 62). Sadie Dayton: Brattleboro Hat (page 78).

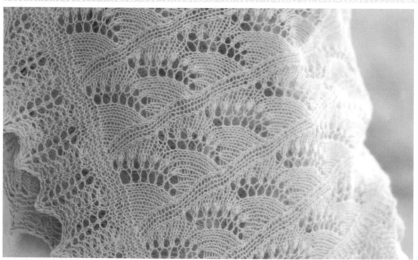

Hourglass
rib socks

by **Chrissy Gardiner**

Finished Size

About 7½" (9, 10½)" (19 [24, 28] cm) foot circumference, 8½ (10, 11)" (21.5 [25.5, 28] cm) foot length from back of heel to tip of toe, and 6 (7, 8)" (15 [18, 20.5] cm) leg length. Socks shown measure 7½" (19 cm) foot circumference.

Yarn

Fingering weight (#1 Super Fine).

Shown here: Classic Elite Alpaca Sox (60% alpaca, 20% merino wool, 20% nylon; 450 yd [411 m]/100 g): #1825 russet, 1 (1, 2) skein(s).

Needles

Size U.S. 1 (2.25 mm): set of 5 double-pointed (dpn).

Adjust needle size if necessary to obtain the correct gauge.

Notions

Cable needle (cn); tapestry needle.

Gauge

6 stitches and 20 rounds = 2" (5 cm) in stockinette stitch, worked in rounds.

The waving cable pattern in Chrissy gardiner's ribbed socks looks like stacked hourglasses or repeating Xs and Os. Either way you look at it, it makes a great pair of socks. The alpaca-blend yarn has a bit of a halo to soften the pattern while adding a luxurious feel. The socks are worked from the top down to the toe, with the ribbed pattern extending along the instep for a comfortable fit.

STITCH GUIDE

C2F

(worked over 2 sts)

Slip 1 st onto cable needle and hold in front, k1, k1 from cable needle.

C2B

(worked over 2 sts)

Slip 1 st onto cable needle and hold in back, k1, k1 from cable needle.

Leg

CO 66 (78, 90) sts. Arrange sts so there are 16 (19, 22) sts on Needle 1, 17 (20, 23) sts on Needle 2, 17 (20, 23) sts on Needle 3, and 16 (19, 22) sts on Needle 4. Join sts for working in rnds, being careful not to twist sts—rnd begins at center of back leg; back-of-leg and bottom-of-foot sts are divided between Needles 1 and 4; front-of-leg and instep sts are divided between Needles 2 and 3.

RNDS 1 AND 2: K2, *p2 (3, 4), k3, p2 (3, 4), k4; rep from * to last 9 (11, 13) sts, p2 (3, 4), k3, p2 (3, 4), k2.

RND 3: C2B (see Stitch guide), *p2 (3, 4), k3, p2 (3, 4), C2F (see Stitch guide), C2B; rep from * to last 9 (11, 13) sts, p2 (3, 4) k3, p2 (3, 4), C2F.

RNDS 4, 5, 6: Rep Rnd 1.

RND 7: C2F, *p2 (3, 4), k3, p2 (3, 4), C2B, C2F; rep from * to last 9 (11, 13) sts, p2 (3, 4), k3, p2 (3, 4), C2B.

RND 8: Rep Rnd 1.

Rep Rnds 1–8 until leg measures about 6 (7, 8)" (15 [18, 20.5] cm) from CO or desired length to top of heel flap, ending with Needle 3 completed on Rnd 4 or 8 of patt.

Heel

Slip 16 (19, 22) sts from Needle 4 onto Needle 1—32 (38, 44) heel sts on one needle; rem 34 (40, 46) instep sts will be worked later when the gussets are picked up.

Heel Flap

Work 32 (38, 44) heel sts back and forth in rows as foll:

ROW 1: (RS) *Sl 1 pwise with yarn in back (wyb), k1; rep from *.

ROW 2: (WS) Sl 1 pwise with yarn in front (wyf), purl to end.

Rep Rows 1 and 2 until heel flap measures 2 (3, 3½)" (5 [7.5, 9] cm) or desired length from beg of flap.

note: *Try on the sock to make sure the flap reaches the base of the heel when the heel touches the ground.*

Turn Heel

Work short-rows as foll:

ROW 1: (RS) Sl 1 pwise wyb, k16 (20, 24), ssk, k1, turn work.

ROW 2: (WS) Sl 1 pwise wyf, p3 (5, 7), p2tog, p1, turn.

ROW 3: Sl 1 pwise wyb, knit to 1 st before gap, ssk (1 st each side of gap), k1, turn.

ROW 4: Sl 1 pwise wyf, purl to 1 st before gap, p2tog (1 st each side of gap), p1, turn.

Rep Rows 3 and 4 until all heel sts have been worked—18 (22, 26) heel sts rem.

Gussets

Pick up sts along selvedge edges of heel flap and rejoin for working in rnds as foll:

RND 1: On Needle 1, K9 (11, 13) to half-way point of heel sts, place marker to denote beg of rnd, k9 (11, 13) rem heel sts, pick up and knit 16 (22, 25) sts along selvedge edge of heel flap; on Needles 2 and 3, work in established patt across 34 (40, 46) instep sts; with empty Needle 4, pick up and knit 16 (22, 25) sts along other selvedge edge of heel flap, then k9 (11, 13) from Needle 1 to marker—84 (106, 122) sts total.

note: *gusset decreases are worked at the end of Needle 1 and the beg of Needle 4 only.*

RND 2: On Needle 1, knit; on Needles 2 and 3, work in established patt across instep sts; on Needle 4, knit to end of rnd.

RND 3: On Needle 1, knit to last 3 sts, k2tog, k1; on Needles 2 and 3, work in established patt; on Needle 4, k1, ssk, knit to end of rnd—2 sts dec'd.

Rep Rnds 2 and 3 until 68 (80, 92) sts rem—17 (20, 23) sts on each needle.

Foot

Working instep sts (Needles 2 and 3) in patt and bottom-of-foot sts (Needles 1 and 4) in St st, cont as established until piece measures about 6½ (7½, 8½)" (16.5 [19, 21] cm) from back of heel, or about 2 (2½, 2¾)" (5 [6.5, 7] cm) less than desired finished length.

Toe

Dec at each side of foot as foll:

RND 1: On Needle 1, knit to last 3 sts, k2tog, k1; on Needle 2, k1, ssk, knit to end of needle; on Needle 3, knit to last 3 sts, k2tog, k1; on Needle 4, k1, ssk, knit to end of rnd—4 sts dec'd.

RND 2: Knit.

Rep Rnds 1 and 2 until 40 (44, 52) sts rem, then rep Rnd 1 only (i.e., dec every rnd) until 16 (20, 20) sts rem.

Finishing

Knit the 4 (5, 5) sts from Needle 1 onto Needle 4 and slip the 4 (5, 5) sts from Needle 3 onto Needle 2—8 (10, 10) sts each on 2 needles. Cut yarn leaving a 12" (30.5 cm) tail. Thread tail on a tapestry needle and use the Kitchener st (see Glossary) to graft live sts tog. Weave in loose ends. Dampen socks and lay flat or place on sock blockers to block.

Echo Reversible
drop-stitch möbius

by **Kristin Omdahl**

Worked in a reversible fabric, this möbius wrap has right and wrong sides that look the same. Dropped stitches showcase the unusual texture of the beautiful yarn and ensure a pretty drape. This project is worked in a flat piece and buttons are placed on the right and wrong sides so that it could be fastened with or without the möbius twist. Twisted and secured, you've got a mobius. Straight and secured with one or two buttons, you've got a capelet. Wrapped twice around the neck and secured with one or two buttons, it's a cowl. Flat and gorgeous all on its own, it's a reversible scarf!

Finished Size

About 10" (25.5 cm) wide and 38" (96.5 cm) long, relaxed after blocking.

Note: The ribbing and dropped stitches make this fabric very stretchy.

Yarn

Chunky weight (#5 Bulky).

SHOWN HERE: Tahki Stacy Charles Loop-D-Loop granite (95% merino, 5% nylon; 55 yd [50 m]/50 g): #002 Mahogany, 4 balls.

Note: This yarn has been discontinued. Please substitute a bulky yarn such as Misti Alpaca Chunky, Berroco Peruvia Quick, or Lion Brand Wool-Ease Thick and Quick. Always remember to check your gauge when substituting yarns.

Needles

Size U.S. 13 (9 mm): 24" (60 cm) circular (cir).

Adjust needle size if necessary to obtain the correct gauge.

Notions

Cable needle (cn); tapestry needle; six 1" (2.5 cm) buttons (buttons shown are JHB #1670 available at www.JoAnn.com).

Gauge

12-stitch cable = 2½" (6.5 cm) wide; dropped stitch = 1¼" (3.2 cm) wide.

Note: This fabric is very stretchy; exact gauge is not critical.

STITCH GUIDE

2/2LC
(worked over 8 sts)

Slip 4 sts onto cn and hold in front of work, work next 4 sts as [k1, p1] 2 times, work 4 sts from cn as [k1, p1] 2 times.

2/2RC
(worked over 8 sts)

Slip 4 sts onto cn and hold in back of work, work next 4 sts as [k1, p1] 2 times, work 4 sts from ch as [k1, p1] 2 times.

Scarf

CO 38 sts.

ROW 1: [K1, p1] 6 times, *k1, [k1, p1] 6 times; rep from * once.

ROWS 2, 3, AND 4: Rep Row 1.

ROW 5: 2/2LC (see Stitch guide), [k1, p1] 2 times, *k1, 2/2LC, [k1, p1] 2 times; rep from * once.

ROWS 6–10: Rep Row 1.

ROW 11: [K1, p1] 2 times, 2/2RC (see Stitch guide), *k1, [k1, p1] 2 times, 2/2RC; rep from * once.

ROW 12: Rep Row 1.

Rep Rows 1–12 ten more times, then rep Rows 1 and 2 once more—piece measures about 37" (94 cm) from CO.

NEXT ROW: (Buttonhole row) [K1, p1] 2 times, k1, BO 2 sts, p1, [k1, p1] 2 times, *k1, [k1, p1] 2 times, k1, BO 2 sts, p1, [k1, p1] 2 times; rep from * once.

NEXT ROW: [K1, p1] 2 times, [(k1, p1) in next st] 2 times, [k1, p1] 2 times, *k1, [k1, p1] 2 times, [(k1, p1) in next st] 2 times, [k1, p1] 2 times.

NEXT ROW: Rep Row 5.

NEXT ROW: Rep Row 1.

Loosely BO 12 sts in patt, draw yarn through st on right-hand needle to fasten off but do not cut yarn, k1; BO next 12 sts in patt, draw yarn through last st on right-hand needle to fasten off but do not cut yarn, k1; BO rem 12 sts in patt and draw yarn through last st and fasten off. Drop rem 2 sts from right needle and ravel to CO edge.

Finishing

Sew three sets of two buttons tog (one on RS and one on WS of fabric, opposite buttonholes) 1" (2.5 cm) in from edge and centered in each of the cable panels. Wrap yarn around the base of each button to form a shank as shown below.

Weave in loose ends. Wet-block and pin to finished measurements. Let air-dry completely before removing pins.

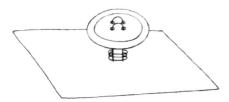

Button Shank Diagram

tip For a larger, luxurious wrap, double the width and length: Cast on 64 stitches (a multiple of 13 stitches plus 12) and knit until the piece is 72" (183 cm) long. But plan for four times as much yarn—880 yards (805 meters)—if you do.

Teak Bittersweet
gauntlets

by **Laura Irwin**

A panel of continuous color changes, both stranded and intarsia, creates a distinct and modern look in these fingerless mitts. A seed-stitch wristband fastened with a leather button completes the look.

Finished Size
8½" (21.5 cm) long, 7½" (19 cm) hand circumference, 5¾" (14.5 cm) wrist circumference. To fit a woman's size small to medium.

Yarn
Fingering weight (Super fine #1).

SHOWN HERE: Rowan 4-ply Soft (100% merino wool; 191 yd [175 m]/50 g): brown mittens, #397 teak (brown; MC) and #396 clover (mauve; CC), 1 ball each; mauve mittens, #396 clover (mauve; MC) and #397 teak (brown; CC), 1 ball each.

Needles
U.S. size 2 (2.75 mm) and U.S. size 1 (2.25 mm).

Adjust needle size if necessary to obtain the correct gauge.

Notions
2 markers (m); sewing needle and matching thread; four ⅝" (1.6 cm) leather buttons; tapestry needle.

Gauge
30 sts and 42 rows = 4" (10 cm) in St st on larger needles; 32 sts and 32 rows = 4" (10 cm) in charted patt on larger needles.

Construction
The mitts are worked flat, following the chart for the color panels. The button straps are knitted separately.

STITCH GUIDE

Bobble

(K1, p1, k1) into same st, turn; p3, turn; sl 1, k2tog, psso.

Hand

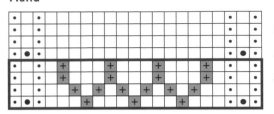

☐ with MC, k on RS, p on WS

• with MC, p on RS, k on WS

+ with CC, k on RS, p on WS

● with MC, make bobble (see Stitch Guide)

☐ pattern repeat

Left Hand

Cuff

With larger needles and MC, CO 71 sts.

ROW 1: (RS) K35, place marker (pm), k1, pm, k35.

ROWS 2-4: Work in St st, slipping markers as you come to them.

ROW 5: K1, ssk, knit to 2 sts before m, k2tog, k1, ssk, knit to last 3 sts, k2tog, k1—4 sts dec'd.

ROWS 6-8: Work even in St st.

Rep Rows 5-8 six more times—43 sts rem.

Remove markers.

Work 8 rows even in St st.

Thumb gusset

ROW 1: (RS; inc row) K1, k1f&b, knit to last 2 sts, k1f&b, k1—2 sts inc'd.

ROW 2: Purl.

Rep Rows 1 and 2 four more times—53 sts.

Work 2 rows even in St st.

[Rep Rows 1 and 2, then work even in St st for 2 rows] 2 times—57 sts.

With MC, k1, M1 (see Glossary), k4, pm, work 21 sts according to Hand chart, pm, knit to end of row—58 sts.

Cont as established, working Hand chart Rows 2-4 between m, then working Hand chart Rows 1-4 between m 5 more times, and working sts outside m in St st.

Change to smaller needles. Work Hand chart Rows 5-8 between m, working sts outside m in St st.

BO all sts.

Right Hand

Work as for left hand to start of chart.

With MC, k31, pm, work 21 sts according to Hand chart, pm, k4, M1, k1—58 sts.

Cont as established, working Hand chart Rows 2-4 between m, then working Hand chart Rows 1-4 between m 5 more times, and working sts outside m in St st.

Change to smaller needles. Work Hand chart Rows 5-8 between m, working sts outside m in St st.

BO all sts.

Strap (make 2)

With MC and larger needles, CO 5 sts.

ROW 1: K1f&b, k1, p1, k1f&b, k1—7 sts.

ROWS 2-13: *K1, p1; rep from * to last st, k1.

ROW 14: (buttonhole row) K1, p1, k1, yo, k2tog, p1, k1.

ROWS 15–31: *K1, p1; rep from * to last st, k1.

Rep buttonhole row.

Work 67 more rows in patt.

NEXT ROW: (bind-off row) K1, ssk, pass knit st over ssk to BO 1 st, p1, pass ssk over purl st to BO 1 st, k2tog, pass purl st over k2tog to BO 1 st, k1, pass k2tog over knit st to BO 1 st. Fasten off last st—no sts rem.

Finishing

Block lightly. With MC threaded on a tapestry needle, use mattress stitch (see Glossary) to sew sides of each mitt from CO edge up 4½" (11.5 cm) and from BO edge down 2½" (6.5 cm), leaving 1½" (3.8 cm) open for thumb.

Strap

With sewing needle and thread, sew one button to RS of plain end of strap. Pull button through second buttonhole. Sew second button to strap to correspond with remaining buttonhole. Weave in loose ends.

Weekend
socks

- -

by **Mags Kandis**

These socks are inspired by classic ski sweaters with traditional crisp, clean, two-color Norwegian motifs. Although the patterns have not changed over the years, the choice of yarns certainly has. The alpaca-bamboo blend used here creates the most scrumptious and decadent pair of socks—just perfect for weekend lounging. Think of them as après-ski sweaters for the feet!

Finished Size
About 8" (20.5 cm) foot circumference and 9" (23 cm) foot length from back of heel to tip of toe. To fit woman's U.S. shoe sizes 7 to 9. Length of foot can be altered to accommodate other shoe sizes.

Yarn
Worsted weight (#4 Medium).
SHOWN HERE: Mirasol Qina (80% baby alpaca, 20% bamboo; 91 yd [83 m]/50 g): #915 (gray) 2 skeins, #900 (natural) and #903 (burnt orange), 1 skein each.

Needles
Size U.S. 5 (3.75 mm): set of 4 double-pointed (dpn).

Adjust needle size if necessary to obtain the correct gauge.

Notions
Marker (m); stitch holder (optional for use during heel shaping); tapestry needle.

Gauge
24 stitches and 24 rounds = 4" (10 cm) in stockinette charted pattern, worked in rounds.

Notes

- *To make it easier to hide the double wrapped stitches during the heel shaping on a purl row, turn the work so that the RS (knit side) is facing you, then pick up the wraps with the left-hand needle and place them on the right-hand needle (see Glossary). Turn work so that the WS (purl side) is facing you and purl the stitch together with the wraps.*

- *Lengthen or shorten foot as needed by working more or fewer rows of the dotted pattern (Rows 53 to 60 of chart) before you begin the toe shaping.*

Left Sock

With gray, CO 48 sts. Divide sts as evenly as possible on 3 dpn. Place marker (pm) and join for working in rnds, being careful not to twist sts. Work in k4, p2 rib for 7 rnds. Work Rnds 1–36 of Weekend Socks chart.

Heel

Sl the previous st knitted onto the next needle, then slip the previous 22 sts onto a holder or waste yarn to work later for instep. Place rem 26 sts onto one needle to work heel.

Change to burnt orange and work short-rows (see Glossary) as foll:

SHORT-ROW 1: (RS) Sl 1, k23, wrap next st, turn.

SHORT-ROW 2: (WS) P22, wrap next st, turn.

SHORT-ROW 3: Knit to 1 st before gap created on previous RS row, wrap next st, turn.

SHORT-ROW 4: Purl to 1 st before gap created on previous WS row, wrap next st, turn.

Weekend socks chart

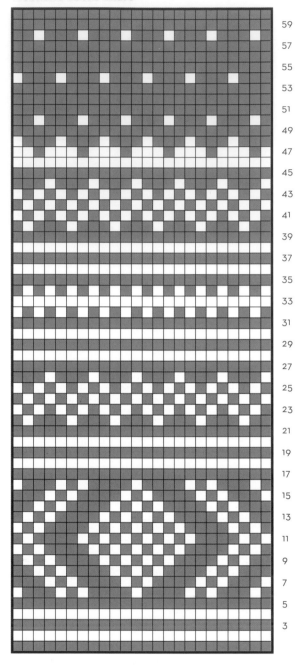

59
57
55
53
51
49
47
45
43
41
39
37
35
33
31
29
27
25
23
21
19
17
15
13
11
9
7
5
3

▦ gray

☐ natural

☐ pattern repeat

SHORT-ROWS 5–14: Rep Short-rows 3 and 4 five more times—10 sts rem unwrapped in center.

SHORT-ROW 15: K10. Knit wrap tog with the next st (see Glossary), wrap the next stitch (this st has 2 wraps), turn.

SHORT-ROW 16: P11. Purl wrap tog with the next st, wrap the next st (this st has 2 wraps), turn.

SHORT-ROW 17: Knit to the first wrapped st, knit the 2 wraps tog with the next st, wrap the next st (this st has 2 wraps), turn.

SHORT-ROW 18: Purl to the first wrapped st, purl the 2 wraps tog with the next st (see Notes), wrap the next stitch (this st has 2 wraps), turn.

SHORT-ROWS 19–28: Rep Short-rows 17 and 18 five more times.

SHORT-ROW 29: K24, knit the 2 wraps tog with the next st, wrap the next st, turn—there is just 1 wrap on this row.

SHORT-ROW 30: P25, purl the 2 wraps tog with the next st, wrap the next st, turn—there is just 1 wrap on this row.

Rejoin for working in rnds (48 sts) and cont as charted until piece measures 6¾" (17 cm) from center of heel or about 2¼" (5.5 cm) less than desired total length (see Notes).

Shape Toe

Change to burnt orange and knit 1 rnd. Dec as folls:

RND 1: *K2tog, k20, ssk; rep from * to end of rnd—44 sts rem.

RNDS 2, 4, 6, 8, 10, AND 12: Knit.

RND 3: *K2tog, k18, ssk; rep from * to end of rnd—40 sts rem.

RND 5: *K2tog, k16, ssk; rep from * to end of rnd—36 sts rem.

RND 7: *K2tog, k14, ssk; rep from * to end of rnd—32 sts rem.

RND 9: *K2tog, k12, ssk; rep from * to end of rnd—28 sts rem.

RND 11: *K2tog, k10, ssk; rep from * to end of rnd—24 sts rem.

RND 13: *K2tog, k8, ssk; rep from * to end of rnd—20 sts rem.

RND 14: Knit.

Finishing

Divide remaining 20 sts equally onto 2 needles. Using the Kitchener st (see Glossary), graft these sts tog. Weave in loose ends. Block lightly if desired.

Right Sock

CO and work as for left sock to beginning of heel. Set up for heel as foll: slip the first st onto the previous needle, then slip the next 22 sts onto a holder or waste yarn to work later for instep. Place rem 26 sts onto one needle to work short-row heel. Beg with Short-row 2, complete as for left sock.

Gentleman's
scarf

by **Véronik Avery**

Véronik Avery designed this manly scarf out of a sumptuous cashmere-silk-blend yarn knitted at a fine gauge. Your fingers will never tire of the feel of the yarn and the simple cables and embossed stitch pattern will hold your interest through every tiny stitch. To make the two sides identical, the scarf is worked in two halves, each beginning with a decorative Channel Island cast-on, which are grafted together at the other ends.

Finished Size
About 8" (20.5 cm) wide and 40½" (103 cm) long.

Yarn
Sportweight (#2 Fine).

SHOWN HERE: Trendsetter Bollicina (65% cashmere, 35% silk; 145 yd [133 m]/50 g): #248 gold, 4 balls.

Note: This yarn has been discontinued. Please substitute any sportweight yarn; suggestions include Road to China Light, 65% baby alpaca, 15% silk, 10% camel + 10% cashmere; Blue Skys Alpacas Alpaca Silk, 50% Alpaca, 50% silk; 146 yd/50 g; Debbie Bliss Baby Cashmerino (55% merino wool, 33% microbifer, 12% cashmere; 137 yd/50 g; 159 yds/50 gram skein; 24-26 sts = 4 inches on US 3-4 Needle. Always remember to check your gauge when substituting yarns.

Needles
Size U.S. 2 (2.75 mm).

Adjust needle size if necessary to obtain the correct gauge.

Notions
Stitch holders; tapestry needle.

Gauge
40 stitches and 52 rows = 4" (10 cm) in charted pattern.

Scarf

First Half

Using the Channel Island method (at right), CO 80 sts. Knit 8 rows. Work Rows 1–12 of Cables & Zigzags chart until piece measures about 20" (51 cm) from CO, ending with Row 1 of chart. Place sts on holder. Cut yarn, leaving a 12" (30.5 cm) tail.

Second Half

CO and work as for first half, ending on Row 11 of chart (instead of Row 1). Cut yarn, leaving a 24" (61 cm) tail.

Finishing

Block pieces lightly. With yarn from second half threaded on a tapestry needle, use the Kitchener st (see Glossary) to graft the live sts of each half tog (or BO the sts for each of the two halves and sew them tog). Weave in loose ends. Block to finished measurements.

Channel Island Cast-on

This cast-on requires three strands of yarn. Use both ends from a center-pull ball (the inner and outer tails) for the double strand and the working end from a second ball for the single strand. Hold the three strands together and make a slipknot, leaving a 4" (10 cm) tail. Place the slipknot on the right needle. The slipknot counts as the first stitch. Wrap the double strands counterclockwise around your thumb two times. Place the remaining single strand over your left finger. The double strands will form the beaded stitches and the single strand will form the regular stitches. *Make a yarnover on the needle with the single strand (**Figure 1**). Hold the yarnover in place on the needle as you insert the needle up through all the loops on your thumb, grab the single strand, and bring it back through the thumb loops (**Figure 2**). Drop the thumb loops and tighten all three yarns to form two more stitches. Repeat from * for the desired number of stitches. Cut the double strands, leaving 4" (10 cm) tails to weave in later and continue to work with the single yarn. *Note: Because the slipknot counts as a stitch, there will be an odd number of stitches. To create an even number of stitches, work two stitches into the slipknot on the first row of knitting.*

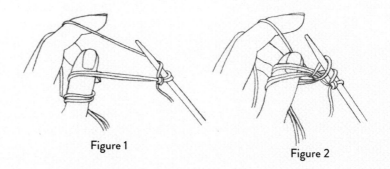

Figure 1   Figure 2

Cables & Zigzags

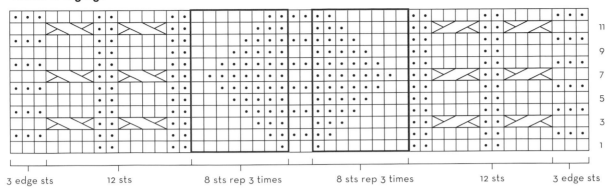

| 3 edge sts | 12 sts | 8 sts rep 3 times | 8 sts rep 3 times | 12 sts | 3 edge sts |

☐ knit on RS; purl on WS

⊡ purl on RS; knit on WS

⧄ 2/2 RC: sl 2 sts onto cable needle and hold in back, k2,k2 from cable needle

⧄ 2/2 LC: sl 2 sts onto cable needle and hold in front, k2, k2 from cable needle

☐ pattern repeat

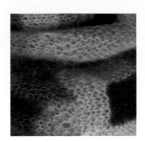

Modern Quilt
wrap

- -

by **Mags Kandis**

What could be more comforting than being wrapped up in the warmth of a colorful quilt? Very loosely based on the traditional Log Cabin quilt block, this wrap/oversized scarf is worked square by square in the easy and satisfying mitered-square method of color knitting. This is as effortless as working in stripes, but the results are far more impressive. As this project is worked one color at a time, it's perfect for thinking about and playing with color.

Finished Size

About 16½" (42 cm) wide and 66" (168 cm) long, after blocking.

Yarn

Sportweight (#2 Fine).

SHOWN HERE: Rowan Kidsilk Haze (70% super kid mohair; 30% silk; 230 yd [210 m]/25 g): #597 jelly (lime green; A), #596 marmalade (orange; B), #583 blushes (rose; C), #600 dewberry (lavender; D), #582 trance (medium blue; E), #578 swish (gold; F), #581 meadow (pale blue; G), #595 liqueur (dark red; H), and #588 drab (grey; I), 1 ball each.

Needles

Size 7 (4.5 mm).

Note: a 16" (40 cm) bamboo circular needle is recommended.

Adjust needle size if necessary to obtain the correct gauge.

Notions

Marker (m); tapestry needle.

Gauge

Small square measures 2¾" (7 cm) square; large square measures 5½" (14 cm) square, both after blocking.

Note

• *Refer to the diagram on page 27 for working order and placement of blocks.*

Small Square

(worked on 24 sts)

ROW 1: (WS) K12, place marker (pm), k12.

EVEN-NUMBERED ROWS 2-20: (RS) Knit to 2 sts before m, k2tog, slip marker (sl m), k2tog through back loops (tbl), knit to end—2 sts dec'd; 4 sts rem after completing Row 20.

ODD-NUMBERED ROWS 3-21: Knit.

ROW 22: K2tog, k2tog tbl—2 sts rem.

Use left needle tip to lift second st on right needle over the first as if to BO—1 st. Cut yarn, draw tail through rem st, and pull tight to fasten off.

Large Square

(worked on 48 sts)

ROW 1: (WS) K24, pm, k24.

EVEN-NUMBERED ROWS 2-44: (RS) Knit to 2 sts before m, k2tog, sl m, k2tog tbl, knit to end—2 sts dec'd; 4 sts rem after completing Row 44.

ODD-NUMBERED ROWS 3-45: Knit.

ROW 46: K2tog, k2tog tbl—2 sts rem.

Use left needle tip to lift second st on right needle over the first as if to BO—1 st. Cut yarn, draw tail through rem st, and pull tight to fasten off.

First Half

Block 1

With A, CO 24 sts. Work Small Square (see Stitch guide), working Rows 1-9 with A and Rows 10-22 with B.

Block 2

With I, CO 12 sts, then pick up and knit 12 sts evenly spaced along side edge of Block 1 as shown in diagram at right—24 sts. Work Small Square, working Rows 1-5 with I, Rows 6-15 with D, and Rows 16-22 with F.

Block 3

With F, pick up and knit 12 sts evenly spaced across top of Block 1, then use the backward-loop method (see Glossary) to CO 12 sts—24 sts total. Work Small Square, working Rows 1-5 with F, Rows 6-13 with E, and Rows 14-22 with H.

Block 4

With C, pick up and knit 12 sts evenly spaced across top of Block 2, then 12 sts evenly spaced along right side of Block 3—24 sts total. Work Small Square, working Rows 1-3 with C, Rows 4-9 with I, and Rows 10-22 with A.

Block 5

With G, CO 24 sts, then pick up and knit 24 sts evenly spaced along right sides of Blocks 2 and 4—48 sts total. Work Large Square (see Stitch guide), working Rows 1-9 with G, Rows 10-17 with H, Rows 18-23 with C, Rows 24-33 with A, and Rows 34-46 with F.

Block 6

With D, CO 24 sts, then pick up and knit 24 sts evenly spaced along right side of Block 5—48 sts total. Work Large Square, working Rows 1-5 with D, Rows 6-15 with B, Rows 16-23 with E, Rows 24-31 with F, and Rows 32-46 with C.

Block 7

With H, CO 24 sts, then pick up and knit 24 sts evenly spaced across top of Block 6—48 sts total. Work Large Square, working Rows 1-9 with H, Rows 10-19 with D, Rows 20-27 with A, Rows 28-33 with G, and Rows 34-46 with B.

Block 8

With E, pick up and knit 12 sts evenly spaced along lower half of left side of Block 7, then pick up and knit 12 sts evenly spaced across first half of top edge of Block 5—24 sts total. Work Small Square, working Rows 1-9 with E and Rows 10-22 with C.

First Half

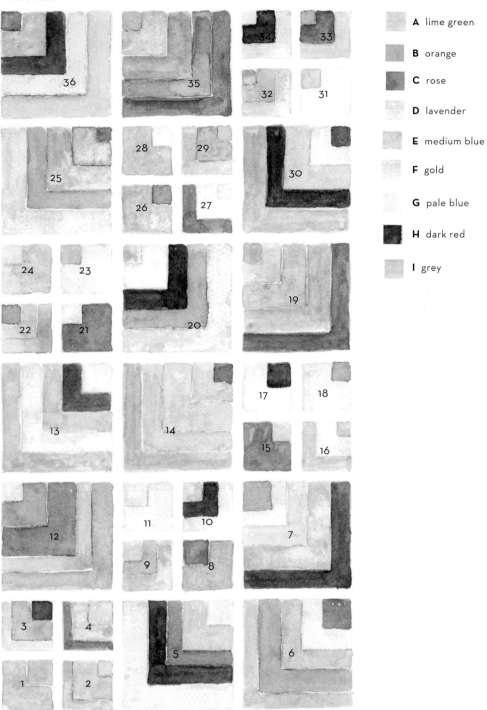

A lime green

B orange

C rose

D lavender

E medium blue

F gold

G pale blue

H dark red

I grey

Block 9

With I, pick up and knit 12 sts evenly spaced along left side of Block 8, then pick up and knit 12 sts evenly spaced across second half of top edge of Block 5—24 sts total. Work Small Square, working Rows 1–5 with I, Rows 6–11 with B, and Rows 12–22 with D.

Block 10

With F, pick up and knit 12 sts evenly spaced along top half of left side of Block 7, then pick up and knit 12 sts evenly spaced along top edge of Block 8—24 sts total. Work Small Square, working Rows 1–5 with F, Rows 6–11 with H, and Rows 12–22 with D.

Block 11

With G, pick up and knit 12 sts evenly spaced along left side of Block 10, then pick up and knit 12 sts evenly spaced along top edge of Block 9—24 sts total. Work Small Square, working Rows 1–9 with G and Rows 10–22 with F.

Block 12

With E, pick up and knit 24 sts evenly spaced along left sides of Blocks 11 and 9, then pick up and knit 24 sts evenly spaced along top edges of Blocks 4 and 3—48 sts total. Work Large Square, working Rows 1–7 with E, Rows 8–13 with A, Rows 14–25 with C, Rows 26–35 with B, and Rows 36–46 with G.

Block 13

With I, pick up and knit 24 st evenly spaced along top edge of Block 12, then use the backward-loop method to CO 24 sts—48 sts total. Work Large Square, working Rows 1–9 with I, Rows 10–17 with F, Rows 18–25 with D, Rows 26–33 with H, and Rows 34–46 with G.

Block 14

With B, pick up and knit 24 sts evenly spaced along top edges of Blocks 10 and 11, then pick up and knit 24 sts evenly spaced along right side of Block 13—48 sts total. Work Large Square, working Rows 1–7 with B, Rows 8–15 with E, Rows 16–27 with A, Rows 28–35 with D, and Rows 36–46 with C.

Block 15

With C, pick up and knit 12 sts evenly spaced along second half of top edge of Block 7, then pick up and knit 12 sts evenly spaced along lower half of right side of Block 14—24 sts total. Work Small Square, working Rows 1–11 with C and Rows 12–22 with A.

Block 16

With I, pick up and knit 12 sts evenly spaced along first half of top edge of Block 7, then pick up and knit 12 sts evenly spaced along right side of Block 15—24 sts total. Work Small Square, working Rows 1–5 with I, Rows 6–13 with F, and Rows 14–22 with E.

Block 17

With F, pick up and knit 12 sts evenly spaced along top edge of Block 15, then pick up and knit 12 sts evenly spaced along top half of right side of Block 14—24 sts total. Work Small Square, working Rows 1–9 with F and Rows 10–22 with H.

Block 18

With g, pick up and knit 12 sts evenly spaced across top edge of Block 16, then pick up and knit 12 sts evenly spaced along right side of Block 17—24 sts total. Work Small Square, working Rows 1–11 with g and Rows 12–22 with B.

Block 19

With C, use the backward-loop method to CO 24 sts, then pick up and knit 24 sts evenly spaced across top edges of Blocks 18 and 17—48 sts total. Work Large Square, working Rows 1-7 with C, Rows 8-17 with I, Rows 18-27 with E, Rows 28-35 with A, and Rows 36-46 with B.

Block 20

With D, pick up and knit 24 sts evenly spaced along right side of Block 19, then pick up and knit 24 sts evenly spaced across top edge of Block 14—48 sts total. Work Large Square, working Rows 1-9 with D, Rows 10-17 with B, Rows 18-25 with H, Rows 26-35 with F, and Rows 36-46 with I.

Block 21

With C, pick up and knit 12 sts evenly spaced along lower half of left side of Block 20, then pick up and knit 12 sts evenly spaced across first half of top edge of Block 13—24 sts total. Work Small Square, working Rows 1-11 with C and Rows 12-22 with F.

Block 22

With A, pick up and knit 12 sts evenly spaced along left side of Block 21, then pick up and knit 12 sts evenly spaced across second half of top edge of Block 13—24 sts total. Work Small Square, working Rows 1-5 with A, Rows 6-11 with D, and Rows 12-22 with B.

Block 23

With G, pick up and knit 12 sts evenly spaced along top half of left side of Block 20, then pick up and knit 12 sts evenly spaced across top edge of Block 21—24 sts total. Work Small Square, working Rows 1-11 with G and Rows 12-22 with D.

Block 24

With E, pick up and knit 12 sts evenly spaced along left side of Block 23, then pick up and knit 12 sts evenly spaced across top edge of Block 22—24 sts total. Work Small Square, working Rows 1-11 with E and Rows 12-22 with A.

Block 25

With F, pick up and knit 24 sts evenly spaced across top edges of Blocks 23 and 24, then use the backward-loop method to CO 24 sts—48 sts total. Work Large Square, working Rows 1-9 with F, Rows 10-17 with B, Rows 18-27 with I, Rows 28-37 with E, and Rows 38-46 with C.

Block 26

With E, pick up and knit 12 sts evenly spaced across second half of top edge of Block 20, then pick up and knit 12 sts evenly spaced along lower half of right side of Block 25—24 sts total. Work Small Square, working Rows 1-11 with E and Rows 12-22 with B.

Block 27

With C, pick up and knit 12 sts evenly spaced across first half of top edge of Block 20, then pick up and knit 12 sts evenly spaced along right side of Block 26—24 sts total. Work Small Square, working Rows 1-5 with C, Rows 6-13 with G, and Rows 14-22 with F.

Block 28

With A, pick up and knit 12 sts evenly spaced across top edge of Block 26, then pick up and knit 12 sts evenly spaced along top half of right side of Block 25—24 sts total. Work Small Square, working Rows 1-11 with A and Rows 12-22 with G.

Block 29

With D, pick up and knit 12 sts evenly spaced across top edge of Block 27, then pick up and knit 12 sts evenly spaced along right side of Block 28—24 sts total. Work Small Square, working Rows 1-5 with D, Rows 6-13 with E, and Rows 14-22 with A.

Block 30

With I, pick up and knit 24 sts evenly spaced across top edge of Block 19, then pick up and knit 24 sts evenly spaced along right sides of Blocks 27 and 29—48 sts total. Work Large Square, working Rows 1-9 with I, Rows 10-17 with H, Rows 18-27 with A, Rows 28-35 with F, and Rows 36-46 with C.

Block 31

With G, CO 12 sts, then pick up and knit 12 sts evenly spaced across first half of top edge of Block 30—24 sts total. Work Small Square, working Rows 1-11 with G and Rows 12-22 with E.

Block 32

With D, pick up and knit 12 sts evenly spaced along left side of Block 31, then pick up and knit 12 sts evenly spaced across second half of top edge of Block 30—24 sts total. Work Small Square, working Rows 1-5 with D, Rows 6-13 with A, and Rows 14-22 with I.

Block 33

With A, CO 12 sts, then pick up and knit 12 sts evenly spaced across top edge of Block 31— 24 sts total. Work Small Square, working Rows 1-5 with A, Rows 6-13 with C, and Rows 14-22 with B.

Block 34

With F, pick up and knit 12 sts evenly spaced along left side of Block 33, then pick up and knit 12 sts evenly spaced across top edge of Block 32—24 sts total. Work Small Square, working Rows 1–5 with F, Rows 6–11 with H, and Rows 12–22 with G.

Block 35

With C, pick up and knit 24 sts along left sides of Blocks 34 and 32, then pick up and knit 24 sts evenly spaced across top edges of Blocks 29 and 28—48 sts total. Work Large Square, working Rows 1–7 with C, Rows 8–15 with B, Rows 16–25 with I, Rows 26–35 with D, and Rows 36–46 with A.

Block 36

With D, pick up and knit 24 sts evenly spaced along left side of Block 35, then pick up and knit 24 sts evenly spaced across top edge of Block 25—48 sts total. Work Large Square, working Rows 1–9 with D, Rows 10–17 with G, Rows 18–25 with H, Rows 26–35 with E, and Rows 36–46 with C.

This completes first half of wrap.

Second Half

Work the first group of blocks for the second half directly onto the top edge of the first half, modifying the block instructions for the first half as foll:

Block 1

With A, pick up and knit 12 sts evenly spaced across second half of top edge of Block 36, then CO 12 sts—24 sts. Work as for Block 1 in first half.

Block 2

With I, pick up and knit 12 sts evenly spaced across first half of top edge of Block 36, then pick up and knit 12 sts evenly spaced along right side of Block 1—24 sts. Work as for Block 2 in first half.

Blocks 3 and 4

Work as for first half.

Block 5

With G, pick up and knit 24 sts evenly spaced across top edge of Block 35, then pick up and knit 24 sts evenly spaced along right sides of Blocks 2 and 4—48 sts total. Work as for Block 5 in first half.

Block 6

With D, pick up and knit 24 sts evenly spaced across top edge of Blocks 33 and 34, then pick up and knit 24 sts along right side of Block 5—48 sts total. Work as for Block 6 in first half.

Blocks 7–36

Work as for first half.

Finishing

Weave in loose ends. Block lightly to measurements.

Vorderrhein
hat

- -

by **Kate Gagnon Osborn**

Twisted-stitch cables—traveling cables comprised of intertwined one-stitch strands in which each stitch is knitted through the back loop—create a tight fabric with beautiful dimension and impressive texture. There is very little information regarding the first occurrence of this special type of cable patterning, but many consider the origin and inspiration to lay in the gnarled trees and deep forests of Germany. The rich pattern in this warm hat begins with a twisted rib that transforms into two alternating cable panels for the longer, slightly slouchy body. The crown is shaped with decreases that are integrated within the cables. A large pom-pom provides a full finish to the top.

Finished Size
About 18¾" (47.5 cm) in circumference and 9¼" (23.5 cm) long, excluding pom-pom. To fit an adult.

Yarn
Worsted weight (#4 Medium).

SHOWN HERE: The Fibre Company Organik (70% organic merino, 15% alpaca, 15% silk; 98 yd [90 m]/50 g): atoll (turquoise), 2 skeins.

Needles
BODY: size U.S. 7 (4.5 mm): 16" (40 cm) circular (cir) and set of 4 or 5 double-pointed (dpn).

RIBBING: size U.S. 5 (3.75 mm): 16" (40 cm) cir.

Adjust needle size if necessary to obtain the correct gauge.

Notions
Markers (m); 2 cable needles (cn); pom-pom maker or cardboard for template; tapestry needle.

Gauge
One cable pattern repeat (24 stitches) = 3¾" (9.5 cm) on larger needles, worked in rounds.

23 rounds = 4" (10 cm) in cable pattern, worked in rounds.

Note
• *Hat can be made without the pompom for a slouchy touque.*

Hat

With smaller cir needle, CO 100 sts. Place marker (pm) and join for working in rnds, being careful not to twist sts. Work Rnd 1 of Ribbing chart 11 times—piece measures about 1½" (3.8 cm) from CO. Work Rnds 2 and 3 of Ribbing chart—120 sts.

Change to larger cir needle.

Work Rnds 1–16 of Cable chart 2 times.

Work Rnds 1–10 of Cable Decrease chart, changing to dpn when there are too few sts to fit comfortably on cir needle—30 sts rem.

NEXT RND: *K1 through back loop (tbl), p1, sl 1 pwise, k2tog, psso, p1; rep from *—20 sts rem.

NEXT RND: *Sl 1 pwise, k1, psso; rep from *—10 sts rem.

Finishing

Cut yarn, leaving an 8" (20.5 cm) tail. Thread tail through rem sts, pull tight to close hole, and fasten off on WS. Block lightly.

Pom-Pom

Make a 2" (5 cm) pom-pom with remaining yarn, using a pom-pom maker or as foll: Cut a piece of cardboard 2" (5 cm) square. Cut a 12" (30.5 cm) length of yarn for tying pom-pom later. Wrap rem yarn around cardboard—more wraps will make a fuller pom-pom. Slide wraps off of cardboard and use 12" (30.5 cm) length to tie tightly at center. Cut loops and fluff pom-pom. Using tails from tying pom-pom, sew pom-pom securely to top of hat. Weave in loose ends.

Cable Knitting Without a Cable Needle

This project is perfect for learning how to work cables without a cable needle, as the vast majority of the cables use only two stitches, which reduces the potential for dropped stitches. For ease of explanation, the directions below describe how to work a 1/1 cable, but the same principles can be applied to cables involving more stitches.

Step 1: Slip the first stitch off of the left-hand needle and let it drop (**Figure 1**) in the front of the work for a left-leaning cable or in the back of the work for a right-leaning cable.

Step 2: Slip the next stitch onto the right-hand needle to temporarily hold it, keeping the dropped stitch in front (**Figure 2**) or back.

Step 3: Return the dropped stitch to the left-hand needle, then return the held stitch from the right-hand needle to the left-hand needle (**Figure 3**).

Step 4: Work these 2 stitches in their new order (**Figure 4**) to complete the cable.

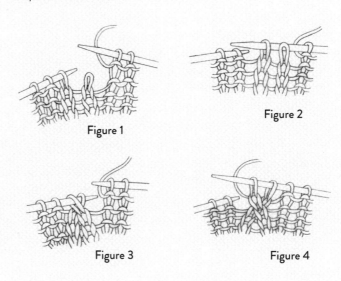

Figure 1

Figure 2

Figure 3

Figure 4

Cable

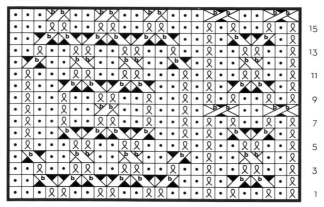

15
13
11
9
7
5
3
1

Cable Decrease

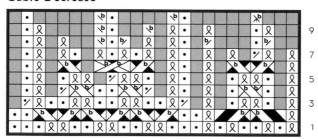

9
7
5
3
1

Ribbing

3
1

k1tbl	k1tbl
·	purl
⅄	p2tog
♭	sl 2 sts pwise, [sl 1 st to left needle by inserting left needle tip from right to left into st] 2 times, k2tog
⅄	k2tog tbl
⁂	sl 1 pwise, k2tog, psso
MP	M1 pwise (see Glossary)
⅄	k1f&b (see Glossary)
▓	no stitch

▢	pattern repeat
⤬	sl 1 st onto cn, hold in back, k1tbl, k1tbl from cn
⤬	sl 1 st onto cn, hold in front, k1tbl, k1tbl from cn
◣	sl 1 st onto cn, hold in back, k1tbl, p1 from cn
◢	sl 1 st onto cn, hold in front, p1, k1tbl from cn
◣	sl 1 st onto cn, hold in back, k1tbl, sl st from cn to left needle, p2tog
⤬	sl 1 st onto cn, hold in back, sl 1 st onto 2nd cn, hold in front, sl st from first cn to left needle, p2tog, k1tbl from cn
⤬	sl 1 st onto cn, hold in back, sl 1 st onto 2nd cn, hold in back, k1tbl, p1 from 2nd cn, k1tbl from first cn

Shaadi
mitts

- -

by **Jaya Srikrishnan**

Inspired by the tradition of Indian brides to decorate their hands with henna patterns and (in North India) wear a lattice of gold chains and medallions, Jaya Srikrishnan designed these intricately patterned fingerless mitts. The backs of the hands are worked in a traditional stranded knitting pattern that mimics a *mehndi* (henna) pattern and the palms are worked in a Bavarian twisted stitch pattern that resembles gold chains. These mitts are a bit challenging to knit, but they'll last a lot longer than a henna tattoo.

Finished Size

About 7 (7¾, 8½)" (18 [19.5, 21.5] cm) circumference and 7 (7½, 8)" (18 [19, 20.5] cm) long. Mitts shown measure 7" (18 cm) in circumference.

Yarn

Fingering weight (#1 Super Fine).

SHOWN HERE: Lorna's Laces Shepherd Sock (100% superwash merino; 215 yd [195 m]/50 g): #37ns violet (A) and #107 red rover (B), 1 skein each.

Needles

Size U.S. 1 (2.25 mm): set of 5 double-point (dpn).

Adjust needle size if necessary to obtain the correct gauge.

Notions

Split-ring or removable markers (m); cable needle (cn); smooth cotton waste yarn; tapestry needle.

Gauge

34 stitches = 2¾" (7 cm) in charted twisted stitch pattern; 34 stitches = 3" (7.5 cm) in charted colorwork pattern; 45 rounds = 4⅛" (10.5 cm) in all charted patterns.

Notes

- *Stretch the stitches on the right needle when changing colors to ensure that the floats are loose enough.*

- *Catch the stranded yarn on the wrong side every 3 stitches or so to prevent long floats—this will allow the color to peek through the front and create the heathered effect. Change the location of where the stranded yarn is caught to prevent vertical lines.*

Right Hand

With A, CO 80 (88, 96) sts. Divide sts, placing 34 sts each on Needles 1 and 3 and 6 (10, 14) sts each on Needles 2 and 4. Attach split-ring marker (pm) into the last st at the end of each needle. Join for working in rnds, being careful not to twist sts.

Cuff

SET-UP RND: On Needles 1 and 3, k1, *p2, [k2, p2] 2 times, k1; rep from * 2 times, pm (see Notes); on Needles 2 and 4, [p2, k2] 1 (2, 3) time(s), p2, pm.

Work sts as they appear (knit the knits and purl the purl for 29 more rnds (30 rnds total) or until piece measures desired length to base of thumb.

Thumb gusset

Join B and work Rnd 1 of Palm chart across 34 sts for palm, slip marker (sl m), k6 (10, 14) with A, sl m, work Rnd 1 of Right Back of Hand chart across 34 sts for back of hand, sl m, k3 (5, 7) with A, pm, use the backward-loop method

Gusset

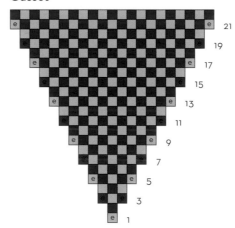

Right Back of Hand

Palm

45
43
41
39
37
35
33
31
29
27
25
23
21
19
17
15
13
11
9
7
5
3
1

45
43
41
39
37
35
33
31
29
27
25
23
21
19
17
15
13
11
9
7
5
3
1

Color A—knit on RS

Color A—purl on RS

Color B—knit on RS

e · increase 1 st using e-wrap (backward loop CO method) and Color A

increase 1 st using e-wrap and Color B

knit 1 st through back loop with Color B

Right Twist—K: sl next st from left needle onto cn, hold in back of work; with color B, k1tbl from left needle, then k1 tbl from cn with color B.

Left Twist—K: sl next st from left needle onto cn, hold in front of work, with color B, k1tbl from left needle, then k1tbl from cn with color B.

Right Twist—K & P: sl next st from left needle onto cn, hold in back; with color B, k1tbl from left needle, then p1 from cn with color A

Left Twist—P & K: sl next st from left needle onto cn, hold in front; with color A, p1 from left needle, then k1tbl from cn with color B.

(see Glossary) to CO 1 st for gusset (this st represents Rnd 1 of gusset chart), pm, k3 (5, 7) with A. Cont working charts as established through Rnd 24 of gusset chart—21 gusset sts between markers.

note: *For a longer gusset, cont in checkerboard patt as established while working Palm and Right Back of Hand charts to the desired length.*

Place 21 gusset sts plus 1 (2, 3) st(s) on each side of gusset on waste yarn holder, removing thumb gusset markers—23 (25, 27) gusset sts on holder; 78 (84, 90) sts rem for hand.

Hand

Work Palm chart across 34 sts, sl m, k6 (10, 14) with A, sl m, work Right Back of Hand chart across 34 sts, sl m, k2 (3, 4) with A, over gap formed by held sts, use the backward-loop method to CO 2 (4, 6) sts with A, k2 (3, 4) with A—80 (88, 96) sts. Cont in patts as established through Rnd 45 of charts. Cut off B. With A only, work rib patt as for cuff until piece measures 7 (7½, 8)" (18 [19, 20.5] cm) from CO. BO all sts in patt.

Thumb

Place 23 (25, 27) held gusset sts on needles. With A, pick up and knit 2 (4, 6) sts along base of CO sts (see Notes), knit to last st, k2tog (last st and first picked-up st), pm, and join for working in rnds—24 (28, 32) sts. Work in k2, p2 rib for 7 (8, 9) rnds or until thumb measures desired length. BO all sts in patt.

Left Hand

CO and work cuff as for right hand.

Thumb gusset

Join B and work Rnd 1 of Left Back of Hand chart across 34 sts for back of hand, sl m, k6 (10, 14) with A, sl m, work Rnd 1 of Palm chart across 34 sts for palm, sl m, k3 (5, 7) with A, pm, use the backward-loop method to CO 1 st for gusset (this st represents Rnd 1 of gusset chart), pm, k3 (5, 7) with A. Cont working charts as established through Rnd 24 of gusset chart—21 gusset sts between markers, or for same length of right-hand gusset. Place 21 gusset sts plus 1 (2, 3) sts on each side of gusset on waste yarn holder, removing thumb gusset markers—23 (25, 27) gusset sts on holder; 78 (84, 90) sts rem for hand.

Hand

Work Left Back of Hand chart across 34 sts, sl m, k6 (10, 14) with A, sl m, work Palm chart across 34 sts, sl m, k2 (3, 4) with A, use the backward-loop method to CO 2 (4, 6) sts with A, k2 (3, 4) with A—80 (88, 96) sts. Cont in patts as established through Rnd 45 of charts. Cut off B. With A only, work rib patt as for cuff until piece measures 7 (7½, 8)" (18 [19, 20.5] cm) from CO. BO all sts in patt.

Thumb

Work thumb as for right hand.

Finishing

Weave in loose ends. Block lightly.

His & Her
socks

by **Ann Budd**

Handknitted socks are always a welcome gift. The patterns on these socks are simple combinations of knit and purl stitches that are interchangeable and easy to modify into other variations. The socks shown here are knitted with machine-washable sportweight merino yarn that is warm and never scratchy. They are worked at a tight gauge that is more typical for fingering-weight yarn to produce a dense well-wearing fabric. Make a pair for everyone in the family!

Finished Size
About 6½ (7, 8)" (16.5 [18, 20.5] cm) foot circumference with rib slightly stretched, 7 (8½, 10)" (18 [21.5, 25.5] cm) foot length from back of heel to tip of toe, and 9 (10¼, 10¼)" (23 [26, 26] cm) leg length from base of heel to top of cuff. To fit a child (woman, man). Blue socks shown measure 7" (18 cm) foot circumference; brown socks shown measure 8" (20.5 cm) foot circumference.

Yarn
Sportweight (#2 Fine).

SHOWN HERE: Louet North America gems Sport Weight (100% merino; 225 yd [206 m]/100 g): 1 (2, 2) skeins. Shown in French blue and ginger.

Needles
Size U.S. 2 (2.75 mm): set of 4 double-pointed (dpn).

Adjust needle size if necessary to obtain the correct gauge.

Notions
Marker (m); tapestry needle.

Gauge
16 stitches and 22 rounds = 2" (5 cm) in stockinette stitch, worked in rounds

STITCH GUIDE

Cuff Pattern

(multiple of 4 sts)

RNDS 1 and **3**: Knit.

RNDS 2 and **4**: Purl.

RNDS 5, 6, AND 7: *K2, p2; rep from *.

RND 8: Purl.

Repeat Rnds 5–8 (do not rep Rnds 1–4) two more times.

Broken Rib Instep Pattern

(worked over 6 sts)

RNDS 1–3 AND 5–7: K2, p2, k2.

RNDS 4, 8, 12 AND 16: Purl.

RNDS 9–11 AND 13–15: P2, k2, p2.

Repeat Rnds 1–16 for pattern.

Leg

CO 52 (60, 68) sts. Place marker (pm) and join for working in rnds, being careful not to twist sts. Work 16 rnds of cuff patt (see Stitch guide). Choose between Checkerboard Rib and Broken Rib charts and work in chosen patt until piece measures about 6 (7¼, 7¼)" (15 [18.5, 18.5] cm) or desired length from CO, ending with Rnd 12 or 15 of Checkerboard Rib chart or Rnd 15, 19, or 23 of Broken Rib chart.

Heel

Divide for heel as foll: K13 (15, 17), turn work.

NEXT ROW: (WS) Sl 1, p25 (29, 33)—26 (30, 34) heel sts on one needle.

Rearrange sts if necessary so that heel sts begin and end with k2 or p2 to ensure that patt is centered on instep. Arrange rem 26 (30, 34) instep sts between 2 needles to work later.

Heel Flap

Work 26 (30, 34) heel sts back and forth in rows as foll:

ROW 1: (RS) *Sl 1 pwise with yarn in back (wyb), k1; rep from *.

ROW 2: (WS) Sl 1 pwise with yarn in front (wyf), purl to end.

Rep Rows 1 and 2 until a total of 26 (30, 34) rows have been worked—13 (15, 17) chain sts along each selvedge edge.

Turn Heel

Work short-rows as foll:

ROW 1: (RS) Sl 1 pwise wyb, k14 (16, 18), ssk, k1, turn work.

ROW 2: (WS) Sl 1 pwise wyf, p5, p2tog, p1, turn work.

ROW 3: Sl 1 pwise wyb, knit to 1 st before gap formed on previous row, ssk (1 st each side of gap), k1, turn work.

ROW 4: Sl 1 pwise wyf, purl to 1 st before gap formed on previous row, p2tog (1 st each side of gap), p1, turn work.

Rep Rows 3 and 4 until all heel sts have been worked, ending with a WS row—16 (18, 20) heel sts rem.

Gussets

Pick up sts along selvedge edges of heel flap and rejoin for working in rnds as foll:

RND 1: With Needle 1, sl 1, k15 (17, 19) to end of heel sts, then pick up and knit 13 (15, 17) sts along

Checkerboard Rib Chart

15
13
11
9
7
5
3
1

Broken Rib Chart

23
21
19
17
15
13
11
9
7
5
3
1

☐ knit on RS; purl on WS

⊡ purl on RS; knit on WS

☐ pattern repeat

selvedge edge of heel flap; with Needle 2, k26 (30, 34) instep in patt as established; with Needle 3, pick up and knit 13 (15, 17) sts along other selvedge edge of heel flap, then knit 8 (9, 10) heel sts from Needle 1—68 (78, 88) sts. Rnd begins at back of heel.

RND 2: On Needle 1, knit to last 2 sts, k2tog; on Needle 2, work instep sts in patt; on Needle 3, ssk, knit to end—2 sts dec'd.

RND 3: Knit.

Rep Rnds 2 and 3 until 52 (60, 68) sts rem—13 (15, 17) sts each on Needle 1 and Needle 3; 26 (30, 34) sts on Needle 2.

Foot

Working bottom-of-foot sts in St st, first 6 and last 6 instep sts in patt as established for checkerboard rib patt or according to Rnds 1–16 of Broken Rib Instep patt (see Stitch guide), and center 14 (18, 22) sts in k2, p2 or p2, k2 rib as desired until foot measures about 5½ (6¾, 8)" (14 [17, 20.5] cm) from back of heel or about 1½ (1¾, 2)" (3.8 [4.5, 5] cm) less than desired total

length, ending with a purl row if working broken rib patt and working this row across all instep sts for a decorative ridge.

Toe

Dec at each side of foot as foll:

RND 1: On Needle 1, knit to last 3 sts, k2tog, k1; on Needle 2, k1, ssk, knit to last 3 sts, k2tog, k1; on Needle 3, k1, ssk, knit to end—4 sts dec'd.

RND 2: Knit.

Rep Rnds 1 and 2 until 28 (32, 36) sts rem, then rep Rnd 1 only (i.e., dec every rnd) until 8 (16, 16) sts rem.

Finishing

Knit the 2 (4, 4) sts from Needle 1 onto Needle 3—4 (8, 8) sts each on 2 needles. Cut yarn leaving a 10" (25.5 cm) tail. Thread tail on a tapestry needle and use the Kitchener st (see Glossary) to graft live sts tog. Weave in loose ends. With yarn threaded on a tapestry needle, tighten up any holes at gussets, if necessary. Block lightly.

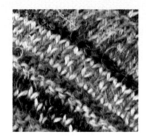

Hued
toque

– –

by **Gudrun Johnston**

The small bands of color in this slouchy hat make for a richly patterned piece that is suitable for a woman or a man. The design provides a foundation that allows you to easily devise a personalized color palette. The quick color changes make it an exciting and addictive knitting technique.

Finished Size
17½" (44.5 cm) circumference at brim; to fit 18–22" (45.5–56 cm) head circumference.

Yarn
Light #3 (DK weight).

SHOWN HERE: Rowan Felted Tweed DK (50% merino wool, 25% alpaca, 25% viscose; 191 yd [175 m]/50 g): #170 seafarer (A), #165 scree (B), #161 avocado (C), #158 pine (D), and #152 watery (E), 1 ball each.

Needles
BRIM: U.S. size 4 (3.5 mm): 16" (40 cm) circular (cir).

BODY: U.S. size 5 (3.75 mm): 16" (40 cm) cir and set of 4 double-pointed (dpn).

Adjust needle sizes if necessary to obtain the correct gauge.

Notions
Marker (m); tapestry needle.

Gauge
26 sts and 36 rnds = 4" (10 cm) in Peerie pattern with larger needles.

Brim

With A and smaller needles, CO 96 sts. Place marker (pm) for beg of rnd and join for working in the rnd, being careful not to twist sts. Purl 1 rnd. Knit 1 rnd. Purl 1 rnd.

Body

Change to larger cir needle. Work Rnds 1–7 of Peerie Chart.

NEXT RND: (inc rnd) With D, *k5, k1f&b; rep from * to end—112 sts.

Work Rnds 9–16 of Peerie Chart.

NEXT RND: (inc rnd) With C, *k6, k1f&b; rep from * to end—128 sts.

Work Rnds 18–23 of Peerie Chart once, then work Rnds 1–23 two more times, then work Rnds 1–16 once more.

Shape Crown

note: *Change to dpns when there are too few sts to work comfortably on cir needle.*

RND 1: With A, *k6, k2tog; rep from * to end—112 sts rem.

RNDS 2, 4, 6, AND 8: Purl.

RND 3: *K5, k2tog; rep from * to end—96 sts rem.

RND 5: *K4, k2tog; rep from * to end—80 sts rem.

RND 7: *K2tog; rep from * to end—40 sts rem.

RND 9: *K2tog; rep from * to end—20 sts rem.

Break yarn, leaving an 8" (20.5 cm) tail. With tail threaded on tapestry needle, draw through rem sts, pull snug to tighten, and fasten off inside.

Finishing

Weave in ends. Soak hat in gentle wool wash and block.

Peerie Chart

	23
	21
	19
	17
	15
	13
	11
	9
	7
	5
	3
	1

- ⊡ purl in same color as previ
- ⊟ Seafarer (A) knit
- △ Scree (B) knit
- ⊞ Avocado (C) knit
- ⊟ Pine (D) knit
- ▢ Watery (E) knit
- ▢ pattern repeat

Carrying Yarns in Fair Isle

When working a piece in Fair Isle, or Peerie pattern as used here, it is very important to make sure that your floats (the strands formed by the nonworking yarn that is carried behind the stitches) aren't too long. When a color needs to be carried for more than four stitches, it is important to wrap the color being carried with the working color every few stitches. This prevents your floats from being too tight and pulling the stitches, or being too loose and easy to snag.

Opera House
mitts

by **Melissa Wehrle**

Finished Size
6" (15 cm) hand circumference (will stretch to about 7½" [19 cm]) and 10½" (26.5 cm) long.

Yarn
Sportweight (#2 Fine).

SHOWN HERE: Bijou Basin Ranch Bijou Spun Lhasa Wilderness (75% yak, 25% bamboo; 180 yd [165 m]/56 g): #01 natural brown, 1 skein.

Needles
MITTS: size U.S. 3 (3.25 mm): double-pointed needles (dpn).

RIBBING: size U.S. 2 (2.75 mm): dpn.

Adjust needle sizes, if necessary, to obtain the correct gauge.

Notions
Markers (m); stitch holder or waste yarn; removable stitch markers or safety pins; tapestry needle; sewing needle and matching thread; two ½" (13 mm) shank buttons.

Gauge
27 sts and 48 rnds in Mock Honeycomb patt on larger needles.

Note
Both mitts are worked the same and can be worn on either hand.

You may or may not have musical talent, but either way, you certainly can make yourself a smart pair of mitts worthy of wearing to any performance. The mock honeycomb pattern is very simple to memorize and moves along rather quickly in the round. This is the perfect project for that luxury skein of yarn you've been holding on to for a special occasion.

STITCH GUIDE

K1, P1 Rib in the Round
(even number of sts)

ALL RNDS: *K1, p1; rep from *.

Rep this rnd for patt.

K1, P1 Rib in Rows
(odd number of sts)

ROW 1: (RS) K1, *p1, k1; rep from *.

ROW 2: (WS) P1, *k1, p1; rep from *.

Rep Rows 1 and 2 for patt.

Mock Honeycomb
(multiple of 4 sts)

Slip all sts purlwise (pwise).

RNDS 1, 3, 5: Knit.

RNDS 2 AND 4: *Sl 3 sts wyf, k1, rep from *.

RND 6: K1, *insert right needle tip under the 2 loose slipped strands from Rnds 2 and 4 and into the next st, knit the next st tog with the strands, k3; rep from *, to last 2 sts, k2.

RND 7: Knit.

RNDS 8 AND 10: K2, *sl 3 sts wyf, k1; rep from * to last 2 sts, sl last 2 sts wyf, sl end-of-rnd marker (m), sl next st wyf (the first st of the foll rnd).

RNDS 9 AND 11: Knit to end of rnd (first st was slipped at end of previous rnd).

RND 12: K3, *insert right needle tip under the 2 loose slipped strands from Rnds 8 and 10 and into the next st, knit next st tog with the strands, k3; rep from * to last st, insert right needle tip under 2 loose strands from Rnds 8 and 10 and into the last st, knit last st tog with the strands.

Rep Rnds 1–12 for patt.

Mitts
Cuff and Lower Hand

With smaller dpn, CO 46 sts. Place marker (pm) and join in the round, being careful not to twist sts. Work in k1, p1 rib in the rnd (see Stitch guide) until cuff measures 1½" (3.8 cm).

Change to larger dpn. Work Rnd 1 of mock honeycomb patt (see Stitch guide) and *at the same time* dec 6 sts evenly spaced—40 sts rem.

Continue in mock honeycomb patt until 66 patt rnds have been completed, ending with Rnd 6 of patt—piece measures 7" (18 cm) from CO.

Thumb gusset

note: *The gusset sts between the thumb markers are worked in St st;*

maintain the mock honeycomb patt as well as possible on each side of the gusset.

SETUP RND (RND 7 OF PATT): K21, pm, k1, pm, k18—1 gusset st between m.

INC RND: Work in patt to first gusset m, sl m, M1 (see Glossary), knit to next gusset m, M1, sl m, work in patt to end—2 gusset sts inc'd.

Work 1 rnd even in patt. Cont in patt, rep the shaping of the last 2 rnds 7 more times—17 gusset sts between m, 56 sts total.

NEXT RND: Work in patt to first gusset m, remove m, place 17 sts on holder, remove m, CO 1 st over gap using the backward-loop method (see Glossary), work in patt to end—40 sts.

Upper Hand

Cont in established patt until Rnds 1–12 of mock honeycomb patt have been worked a total of 8 times, then work Rnds 1–6 once more—102 patt rnds total; piece measures 10" (25.5 cm) from CO.

Change to smaller needles. Knit 1 rnd, inc 6 sts evenly spaced—46 sts.

Work in k1, p1 rib in the rnd for 4 rnds—piece measures 10½" (26.5 cm) from CO. BO all sts using the tubular k1, p1 rib BO method (see Glossary).

Finishing
Thumb

Place 17 held thumb sts on larger dpn and distribute as evenly as possible on 3 dpn. Join yarn to beg of sts with RS facing.

NEXT RND: K17, pick up and knit 1 st from base of st CO across thumb gap—18 sts.

Knit 1 rnd. Work k1, p1 rib in the rnd for 4 rnds. BO all sts using the tubular k1, p1 rib BO method (see Glossary). Work second thumb in the same manner.

Button Tabs (make 2)

With 2 smaller dpn, CO 9 sts. Working back and forth in rows, work in St st for 4 rows. Change to k1, p1 rib in rows (see Stitch guide) and work in rib patt until tab measures 2¼" (5.5 cm) from CO, ending with a WS row.

DEC ROW: (RS) Ssk, work in patt to last 2 sts, k2tog—2 sts dec'd.

Cont in patt, rep the dec row on the next 2 RS rows, then work 1 WS row even—3 sts rem.

NEXT ROW: (RS) Sl 2 sts as if to k2tog, k1, pass 2 slipped sts over—1 st rem.

Cut yarn and fasten off last st. Work a second tab in the same manner.

Block mitts and button tabs. Weave in ends.

Try mitts on and use removable markers or safety pins to position button tabs at CO edges of mitts where they look best to you. For the mitts shown, the tabs are attached to the pinky side of each mitt, opposite the thumb gussets. Fold the St st section of each tab around the CO edge of the mitt so only the ribbed portion of the tab shows on the RS of the mitt. Using sewing needle and thread, sew CO edge of each tab invisibly to WS of mitt. Sew a button about 1" (2.5 cm) from the pointed end of each tab as shown, sewing through both layers of the tab and mitt.

Caitlin Cabled
scarf

•– – – – – – – – – – – – – – – – – –•

by **Connie Chang Chinchio**

Finished Size
About 10½" (26.5 cm) wide and 67" (170 cm) long, after blocking.

Yarn
Worsted weight (#4 Medium).

SHOWN HERE: Quince and Company Osprey (100% wool; 170 yd [155 m]/100 g): lichen, 4 skeins.

Needles
U.S. size 9 (5.5 mm).

Adjust needle size if necessary to obtain the correct gauge.

Notions
Cable needle (cn); tapestry needle.

Gauge
20 sts and 24½ rows = 4" (10 cm) in cable patt from chart.

For scarves, it's important to choose a yarn that's soft enough to wear against the skin and hardy enough for everyday use. Both soft and lofty, Quince and Company's Osprey is ideal for this densely cabled scarf. Interlocking cables meander along the length, but the stitch pattern is actually quite easy to memorize. After several repeats, you'll find yourself putting away the chart and simply reading the stitches as you go.

Scarf

CO 52 sts. Rep Rib Rows 1 and 2 of Cable chart until piece measures 3" (7.5 cm) from CO when stretched to 10½" (26.5 cm) wide, ending with WS Rib Row 2. Work Rows 1–36 of chart 10 times (do not rep the rib rows), then work Rows 1–14 once more—374 rows completed from main section of chart. Rep Rib Rows 1 and 2 until ribbed section measures 3" (7.5 cm) long when stretched to 10½" (26.5 cm) wide (i.e., work the same number of rows as at the beg). Loosely BO all sts.

Finishing

Block lightly. Weave in loose ends.

Cable

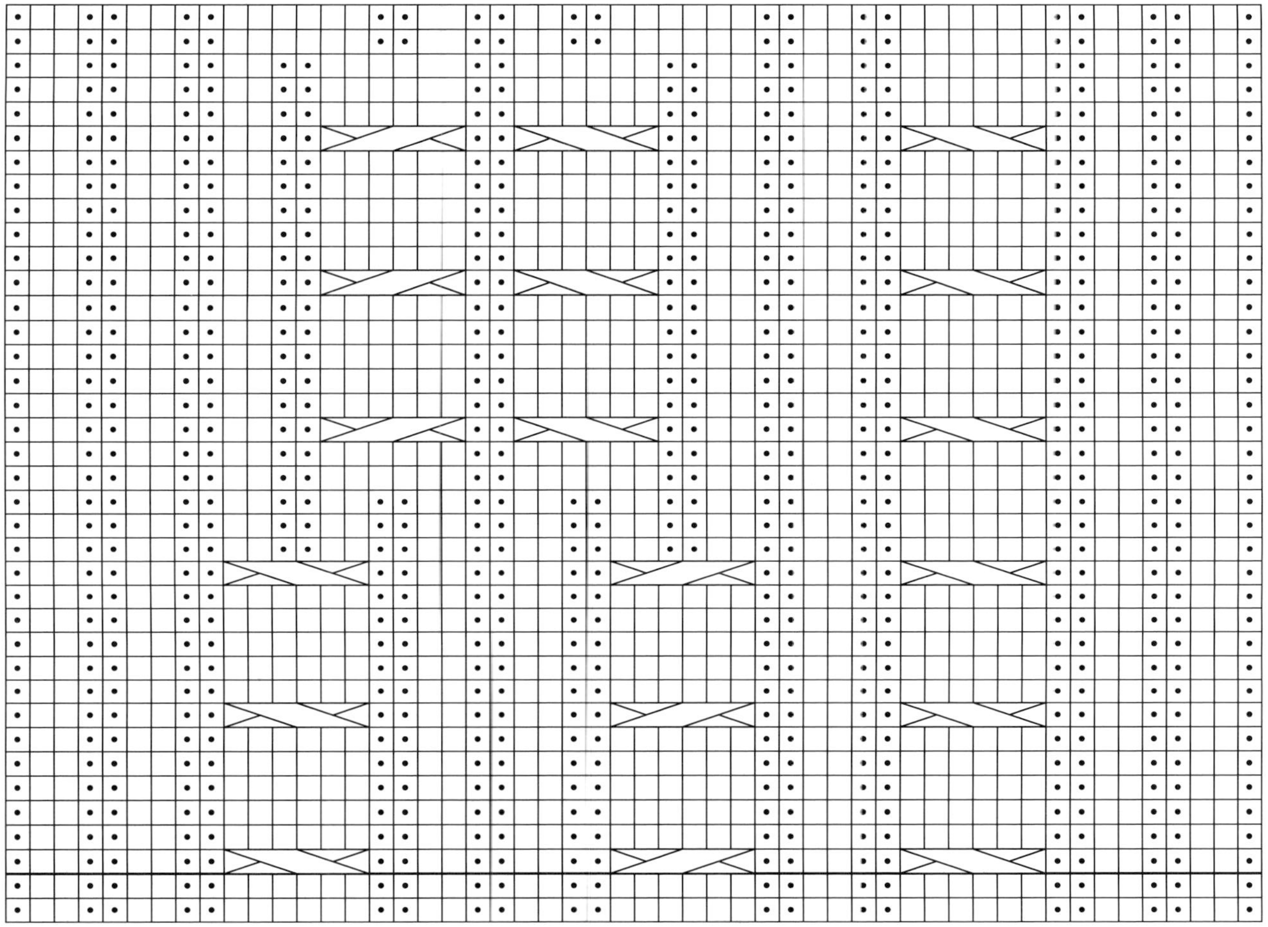

35 33 31 29 27 25 23 21 19 17 15 13 11 9 7 5 3 1 Rib Row 1

Rib Row 2

knit on RS; purl on WS

purl on RS; knit on WS

3/3RC: sl 3 sts onto cn and hold in back, k3, k3 from cn

3/3LC: sl 3 sts onto cn and hold in front, k3, k3 from cn

Wanderer
cap

– –

by **Jared Flood**

Finished Size
21¼" (54 cm) circumference at widest point, unstretched; to fit head circumference 20–23" (51–58.5 cm).

Yarn
Medium #4 (worsted weight).

SHOWN HERE: Brooklyn Tweed Shelter (100% American wool; 140 yd [128 m]/50 g): #04 hayloft, 1 skein.

Needles
RIBBING: U.S. size 7 (4.5 mm): 16" (40 cm) circular (cir).

BODY: U.S. size 8 (5 mm): 16" (40 cm) cir and set of 4 double-pointed (dpn).

Adjust needle sizes if necessary to obtain the correct gauge.

Notions
Marker (m); cable needle (cn); tapestry needle, waste yarn.

Gauge
18 sts and 36 rnds = 4" (10 cm) in garter st on larger needle.

Knit with a rustic tweed yarn, this quick-to-stitch, classic cap features a zigzag pattern that adds a simple yet bold detail that's perfect for the men in your life. The design flows seamlessly from the ribbed band, for a flawless finished look.

Left Twist (LT)

Sl 1 st onto cn and hold in front, k1 from left needle, k1 from cn.

Right Twist (RT)

Sl 1 st onto cn and hold in back, k1 from right needle, k1 from cn.

Ribbing

With smaller cir needle and using tubular method (see Glossary), CO 88 sts. Place marker (pm) and join for working in the rnd, being careful not to twist sts.

RND 1: *K1, p1; rep from * to end.

Rep last rnd until piece measures 1" (2.5 cm).

Body

NEXT RND: (inc rnd) *K14, M1 (see Glossary), k30, M1; rep from * once more—92 sts.

NEXT RND: *Sl 1 purlwise (pwise) with yarn in back (wyb), p1, sl 1 pwise wyb, p12, sl 1 pwise wyb, p1, sl 1 pwise wyb, p13, sl 1 pwise wyb, p1, sl 1 pwise wyb, p12; rep from * once more.

Change to larger cir needle.

NEXT RND: (inc rnd) LT (see Stitch guide) 2 times, k11, M1, LT 2 times, k12, LT 2 times, k11, m1; rep from * once more, remove m, sl 1 pwise wyb, pm for beg of rnd—96 sts.

Work Rnds 1–14 of Silo Chart moving the marker at the end of each even numbered rnd.

NEXT RND: Work Rnd 15 to end of rnd. Remove m, slip 3 sts from left to right needle, pm for new beg of rnd.

NEXT RND: Work Rnd 16 to last 2 sts of rnd, sl 1 st to cn, hold in back, k1, slip beg of rnd m, return st on cn to left needle unworked.

Work Rnds 17–31 of Silo chart, ending every even-numbered rnd as for Rnd 16 (moving marker).

Shape Crown

note: *Change to dpns when there are too few sts to work comfortably on cir needle.*

Work Rnds 32–56 of Silo chart, decreasing 6 sts on every even-numbered rnd as indicated—18 sts rem.

Break yarn, leaving a 6" (15 cm) tail. With tail threaded on tapestry needle, draw through rem sts, pull snug to tighten, and fasten off inside.

Finishing

Weave in ends. Steam- or wet-block.

Silo Chart

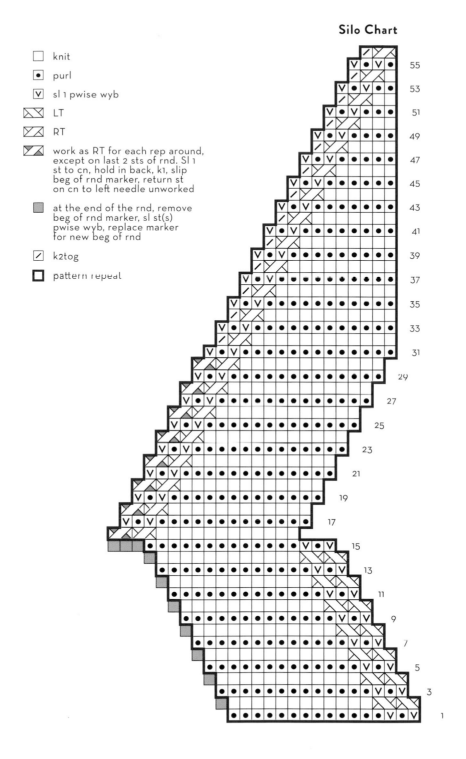

knit

• purl

V sl 1 pwise wyb

LT

RT

work as RT for each rep around, except on last 2 sts of rnd. Sl 1 st to cn, hold in back, k1, slip beg of rnd marker, return st on cn to left needle unworked

at the end of the rnd, remove beg of rnd marker, sl st(s) pwise wyb, replace marker for new beg of rnd

k2tog

pattern repeat

Jasmin
headscarf

- -

by **Kristeen Griffin-Grimes**

The twining green leaves of the night-blooming jasmine (Jasminum sambac) provided the inspiration for this easy-to-wear headwrap. The verdantly colored lightweight yarn with burnished metallic accents harkens back to the bohemian sentiments of the 1970s.

Finished Size
About 22" (56 cm) head circumference, tied, and about 11" (28) wide in lace section.

Yarn
Worsted weight (#4 Medium).

SHOWN HERE: Berroco glint (80% cotton, 12% nylon, 8% metallic; 141 yd [129 m]/50 g); #2940 Alexander (olive), 2 skeins.

Note: This yarn has been discontinued. Please substitute any worsted weight yarn such as Berroco Maya (85% cotton, 15% Alpaca; 137 yds [125 m]/50 g). Always remember to check your gauge when substituting yarns.

Needles
Size U.S. 7 (4.5 mm): straight or 16" (40 cm) circular (cir).

Adjust needle size if necessary to obtain the correct gauge.

Notions
Smooth cotton waste yarn for provisional cast-on; markers (m); removable markers; stitch holders; tapestry needle.

Gauge
21 sts and 24 rows = 4" (10 cm) in patt from Leaf chart.

First Half

Leaf Lace Section

With waste yarn and using a provisional method (see Glossary), CO 58 sts. Work the WS set-up row of Leaf chart once, then rep Rows 1–12 four times (do not rep the set-up row), then work Rows 1–3 once more, ending with a RS row—52 chart rows completed; piece measures about 8¾" (22 cm) from CO. Cut yarn, leaving a 24" (61 cm) tail for grafting. Place sts on holder.

Tie

Carefully remove waste yarn from provisional CO and place 58 live sts on needle. Join yarn with RS facing, ready to begin with a RS row.

ROW 1: (RS) Knit, correcting any st mounts if necessary.

ROW 2: (WS) [P2tog, yo] 14 times, k2tog, [yo, p2tog] 14 times—57 sts rem.

ROW 3: Knit.

ROW 4: [P2tog] 14 times, k1, [p2tog] 14 times—29 sts rem.

ROW 5: K2, [k2tog] 6 times, k1, [k2tog] 6 times, k2—17 sts rem.

ROW 6: [P2tog, yo] 4 times, k1, [yo, p2tog] 4 times.

ROW 7: Knit.

Rep Rows 6 and 7 fourteen more times, then work WS Row 6 once more—tie measures about 6" (15 cm) from last row of Leaf chart.

Dec for tip as foll:

ROW 1: (RS) [Ssk] 2 times, k9, [k2tog] 2 times—13 sts rem.

ROW 2: (WS) [P2tog, yo] 3 times, k1, [yo, p2tog] 3 times.

ROW 3: [Ssk] 2 times, k5, [k2tog] 2 times—9 sts rem.

ROW 4: [P2tog, yo] 2 times, k1, [yo, p2tog] 2 times.

ROW 5: [Ssk] 2 times, k1, [k2tog] 2 times—5 sts rem.

ROW 6: P2tog, yo, k1, yo, p2tog.

ROW 7: Ssk, k1, k2tog—3 sts rem.

ROW 8: P3tog—1 st rem; tie measures about 7½" (19 cm) from last row of Leaf chart.

Cut yarn and fasten off rem st.

Second Half

Work lace section and tie as for first half—58 live sts rem on holder.

Finishing

Temporarily pin the live sts at the ends of the two halves tog and try on for fit. If necessary, adjust the length by adding or removing the same number of rows in each half, making sure to end each piece with a RS row. Every 2 rows added or removed in both halves (4 rows total) will lengthen or shorten the entire headwrap by about ¾" (2 cm). With yarn threaded on a tapestry needle, use the Kitchener st for St st (see Glossary) to graft the sts tog, taking care to include the yarnovers in each side border.

Weave in loose ends. Wet-block (see Glossary) to measurements.

Leaf

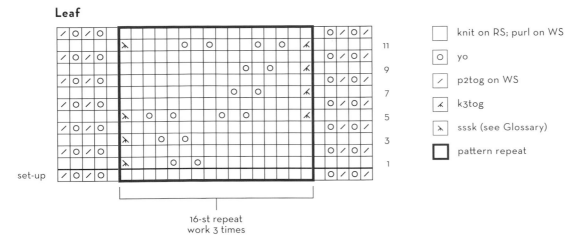

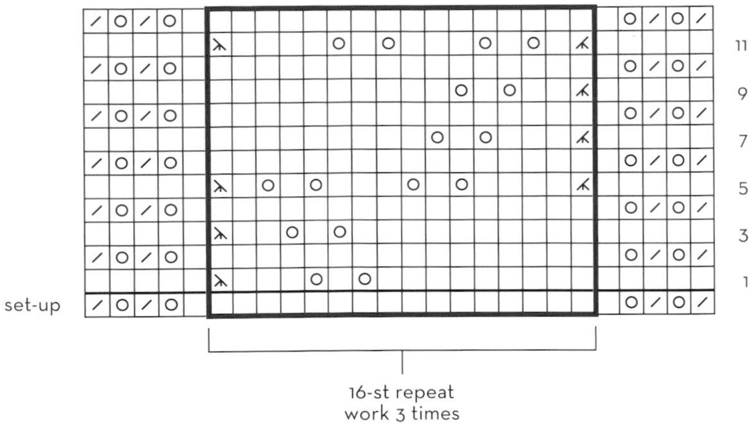
11
9
7
5
3
1
set-up
16-st repeat
work 3 times

- knit on RS; purl on WS
- yo
- p2tog on WS
- k3tog
- sssk (see Glossary)
- pattern repeat

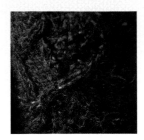

McIntosh
boot socks

- -

by **Jennifer Burke**

The cables in these socks evoke windswept, winding roads—perfect for an afternoon of "leaf-peeping" in the countryside. The alpaca content in the Felted Tweed yarn softens the look of the cables and seed stitch without compromising stitch definition or texture. The legs are tapered along the sides in the seed-stitch panels so that the cable panel remains intact. The result is a streamlined look with a perfect fit!

Finished Size

About 8¾" (22 cm) foot circumference, slightly stretched, 9½" (24 cm) foot length, and 10¼" (26 cm) upper leg circumference.

To fit women's U.S. size 8 to 10 shoe.

Yarn

DK weight (#3 Light).

SHOWN HERE: Rowan Felted Tweed DK (50% merino wool, 25% alpaca, 25% viscose; 191 yd [175 m]/50 g): #150 rage, 2 balls.

Needles

LEG AND FOOT: size U.S. 4 (3.5 mm): set of 4 or 5 double-pointed (dpn).

RIBBING: size U.S. 3 (3.25 mm): set of 4 or 5 dpn.

Adjust needle size if necessary to obtain the correct gauge.

Notions

Markers (m); cable needle (cn); tapestry needle.

Gauge

24 sts and 36 rnds = 4" (10 cm) in St st on larger needles, worked in rnds.

28 sts in cable patt = 3½" (9 cm) on larger needles, worked in rnds.

STITCH GUIDE

Seed Stitch

(multiple of 2 sts)

RND 1: *P1, k1; rep from *.

RND 2: *K1, p1; rep from *.

Rep Rnds 1 and 2 for patt.

Leg

With smaller needles, CO 76 sts. Divide sts on 3 or 4 dpn, place marker (pm), and join for working in rnds, being careful not to twist sts.

Work in k2, p2 rib until piece measures 2½" (6.5 cm) from CO.

Change to larger needles.

SET-UP RND: Work Rnd 1 of Cable chart (see page 69) over 28 sts, pm, work 10 sts in seed st (see Stitch guide), pm, work Rnd 1 of Cable chart over 28 sts, pm, work 10 sts in seed st.

Keeping in patt and slipping markers (sl m) when you come to them, work through Rnd 15 of chart.

DEC RND: (Rnd 16 of chart) *Work 28 sts as charted, k2tog or p2tog as necessary to maintain patt, work in seed st to 2 sts before m, ssk or ssp (see Glossary) as necessary to maintain patt; rep from * once—4 sts dec'd.

Work Rnds 17–20 of chart.

Rep the last 20 rnds 3 more times, working decs on each rep of Rnd 16 and ending the last rep of the last rnd 1 st before end-of-rnd m—60 sts rem (2 seed sts between each set of markers); piece measures about 11½" (29 cm) from CO.

Heel

Beg with last st from previous rnd, work 30 sts for heel as foll: K1, k1tbl, p2, k1, ssk, [k1, p1] 2 times, k1, p2tog, k2, ssp, [k1, p1] 2 times, k1, k2tog, k1, p2, k1tbl, k1—26 sts rem for heel flap; rem 30 sts will be worked later for instep.

Heel Flap

Work 26 heel sts back and forth in rows as foll:

ROW 1: (WS) Sl 1 purlwise with yarn in front (pwise wyf), p1 through back loop (p1tbl), k2, p2, [k1, p1] 3 times, p2, [p1, k1] 3 times, p2, k2, p1tbl, k1.

ROW 2: (RS) Sl 1 pwise with yarn in back (wyb), k1tbl, p2, k2, [k1, p1] 3 times, k2, [p1, k1] 3 times, k2, p2, k1tbl, k1.

Rep these 2 rows 11 more times, then work Row 1 once again—26 rows total; 13 slipped chain sts along each selvedge.

Turn Heel

Work short-rows to shape heel as foll:

ROW 1: (RS) Sl 1 pwise wyb, k14, ssk, k1, turn work.

ROW 2: (WS) Sl 1 pwise wyf, p5, p2tog, p1, turn work.

ROW 3: (RS) Sl 1 pwise wyb, knit to 1 st before gap made on previous row, ssk, k1, turn work.

ROW 4: (WS) Sl 1 pwise wyf, purl to 1 st before gap made on previous row, p2tog, p1, turn work.

Rep Rows 3 and 4 until all sts have been worked, ending with a WS row—16 sts rem.

Cable

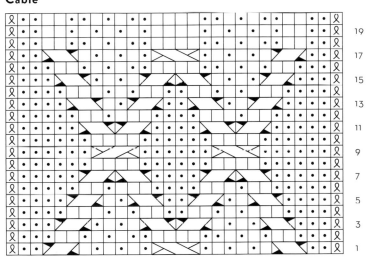

19

17

15

13

11

9

7

5

3

1

☐ knit

⦁ purl

Ⱦ k1 through back loop (tbl)

sl 1 onto cn and hold in back, k2, p1 from cn

sl 2 onto cn and hold in front, p1, k2 from cn

sl 2 onto cn and hold in back, k2, k2 from cn

sl 2 onto cn and hold in front, k2, k2 from cn

Gussets

With RS facing, k8, pm for new beg of rnd, k8, pick up and knit 14 sts along side of heel flap (13 heel flap sts plus 1 st in the corner between the flap and instep), pm, p1, k1tbl, p2tog, k2, [p1, k1] 3 times, p1, ssk, k2tog, [p1, k1] 3 times, p1, k2, p2tog, k1tbl, p1, pm, pick up and knit 14 sts along other side of heel flap as before, then knit 8 sts from bottom of foot to end of rnd—70 sts total.

SET-UP RND: K8, k14tbl, p1, k1tbl, p1, k2, [k1, p1] 3 times, k4, [p1, k1] 3 times, k2, p1, k1tbl, p1, k14tbl, k8.

Keeping 7 sts in seed st at each side of instep as established, dec gussets as foll:

RND 1: Knit to 3 sts before m, k2tog, k1, sl m, work patt as established across 26 instep sts, sl m, k1, ssk, knit to end—2 sts dec'd.

RND 2: Work even in patt as established.

Rep these 2 rnds 8 more times—52 sts rem.

Foot

Work even in pattern as established until piece measures about 7½" (19 cm) from back of heel, or about 2" (5 cm) less than desired total length.

Toe

Work all sts in St st as foll:

RND 1: *Knit to 3 sts before m, k2tog, k1, sl m, k1, ssk; rep from * once, then knit to end of rnd—4 sts dec'd.

RND 2: Knit.

Rep these 2 rnds 8 more times—16 sts rem; 8 sts each for instep and bottom of foot.

Place each set of 8 sts onto a separate needle.

Finishing

Cut yarn, leaving a 12" (30.5 cm) tail. Thread tail on a tapestry needle and use the Kitchener st (see Glossary) to graft rem sts tog.

Weave in loose ends. Block lightly if desired.

Madeleine
shawl

— — — — — — — — — — — — — — — — — —

by **Courtney Kelley**

Finished Size
About 54" (137 cm) wide and 24" (61 cm) long at point.

Yarn
Worsted weight (#4 Medium).

SHOWN HERE: The Fibre Company Road to China (65% baby alpaca, 15% silk, 10% camel, 10% cashmere; 69 yd [63 m]/50 g): jade, 4 skeins.

Needles
Size U.S. 10 (6 mm).

Adjust needle size if necessary to obtain the correct gauge.

Notions
Tapestry needle.

Gauge
About 11 stitches and 18 rows = 4" (10 cm) in bias-stitch pattern.

This pretty picot-edged shawl is a great traveling or weekend project. It is knitted point to point in a garter-based bias-stitch pattern that is worked simultaneously with the picot edge. The construction is simple enough for beginners and interesting enough to keep advanced knitters engrossed. The bias pattern creates a Faroese-style wing to shape the points, which allows the shawl to drape comfortably around the shoulders. Knitted in a worsted-weight luxury yarn, this shawl mixes the practical warmth of a thick homespun peddler's shawl with the softness of a fine Regency-era cashmere shawl.

STITCH GUIDE

Make Picot (MP)

Using the cable method (see Glossary), CO 3 sts. Working the first st through the back loop, BO 3 sts.

Shawl

CO 2 sts.

SET-UP ROW 1: K1f&b (see Glossary), k1—3 sts.

SET-UP ROW 2: [K1f&b] 2 times, k1—5 sts.

Cont to inc in patt as foll:

ROW 1: Sl 1, *ssk, yo; rep from * to last 2 sts, k2.

ROW 2: MP (see Stitch Guide), k1f&b, knit to end—1 st inc'd.

ROW 3: Sl 1, *ssk, yo; rep from * to last 3 sts, k3.

ROW 4: K1f&b, knit to end—1 st inc'd.

Rep these 4 rows 29 more times, ending with Row 4—65 sts, 30 picots; piece measures about 27" (68.5 cm) from CO.

Dec in patt as foll:

ROW 1: Sl 1, k1, *yo, ssk; rep from * to last 3 sts, k3.

ROW 2: MP, ssk, knit to end—1 st dec'd.

ROW 3: Sl 1, k1, *yo, ssk; rep from * to last 2 sts, k2.

ROW 4: Ssk, knit to end—1 st dec'd.

Rep these 4 rows 29 more times, ending with Row 4—5 sts rem.

NEXT ROW: Sl 1, k1, yo, ssk, k1.

NEXT ROW: Ssk, k3—4 sts rem.

NEXT ROW: Ssk, k2tog—2 sts rem.

BO rem 2 sts.

Finishing

Weave in loose ends. Steam-block to measurements.

Designing Bias-Stitch Patterns

In woven fabrics, the lengthwise grain is the direction of the warp threads that run vertically along the fabric, and the widthwise grain is the direction of the weft threads that run horizontally across the fabric. The bias is measured at 45 degrees to the vertical and horizontal, or diagonally across the fabric. Garments constructed on the bias will have more stretch and hang with more drape than garments constructed on the lengthwise or widthwise grain. Knitted fabrics can also be constructed on the bias to maximize drape. Achieved through the creative use of increases on one side of the work paired with decreases on the other side, a rectangular fabric can be created in which the stitches slant to the left or right. The increases add fabric to one edge while the decreases remove fabric from the other. This produces a fabric that hangs beautifully and is particularly effective for shawls and wraps.

The direction of bias depends on the placement of the increases and decreases. If the increases are worked at the beginning of right-side rows and the decreases are worked at the end these rows, the fabric will slant toward the left. If the increases are worked at the end of right-side rows and the decreases are worked at the beginning of these rows, the fabric will slant toward the right.

The stitch pattern for the first half of this shawl is a simple repetition of ssk decreases followed by yarnover increases.

Row 1: (RS) K1, *ssk, yo; rep from * to last 2 sts, k2.

Row 2: (WS) Knit.

As these two rows are repeated, the yarnover increases and ssk decreases align vertically to form pillars. Because the decreases are worked before the increases, the fabric slants to the left.

For the second half of the shawl, the yarnover increases are followed by ssk decreases.

Row 1: (RS) K2, *yo, ssk; rep from * to last st, k1.

Row 2: (WS) Knit.

As these two rows are repeated, the fabric slants to the right because the increases are worked before the decreases.

A "V" forms where the stitch pattern changes direction, which is perfectly formed to cradle the nape of your neck.

Brattleboro
hat

— · — · — · — · — · — · — · — · — · — · — · — · —

by **Melissa LaBarre**

Finished Size

20" (51 cm) circumference at band.

Yarn

Worsted (Medium #4).

SHOWN HERE: Malabrigo Merino Worsted (100% wool; 215 yd [197 m]/100 g): #117 verde adriana, 1 skein.

Needles

U.S. size 8 (5 mm): 16" (40 cm) circular (cir) and set of 4 or 5 double-pointed (dpn).

Adjust needle size if necessary to obtain the correct gauge.

Notions

Markers (m); two 1" (2.5 cm) buttons; tapestry needle.

Gauge

18 sts and 25 rnds = 4" (10 cm) in moss st.

22 sts and 25 rows = 4" (10 cm) in k2, p2 rib, relaxed.

This hat is knitted in two directions: a ribbed band is worked from side to side to create the brim, and stitches are picked up along one side for the moss stitch crown. A button tab at the side gives this simple design a twist.

Moss Stitch

(multiple of 2 sts)

RNDS 1 AND 2: *K1, p1; rep from * to end.

RNDS 3 AND 4: *P1, k1; rep from * to end.

Rep Rnds 1–4 for patt.

Hat

Ribbed Band

With cir needle, CO 20 sts. Do not join.

ROW 1: (RS) K3, *p2, k2; rep from * to last 5 sts, p2, k3.

ROW 2: Work sts as they appear.

Rep Rows 1 and 2 until piece measures 20" (51 cm) from CO, ending with a WS row. BO all sts in patt. Block piece to relax rib.

Body

With cir needle and RS facing, pick up and knit (see Glossary) 80 sts evenly spaced along one long edge of ribbed band. Place marker (pm) and join for working in the rnd.

Work Rnds 1–4 of moss st (see Stitch Guide) 3 times, then work Rnds 1–3 once more—15 rnds total.

NEXT RND: Cont in patt, *work 20 sts, pm; rep from * 3 more times.

Shape Crown

NEXT RND: (dec rnd) *K2tog, work in patt to 2 sts before m, ssk; rep from * 3 more times—8 sts dec'd.

Rep dec rnd every other rnd 7 more times, maintaining patt between m—16 sts rem.

Work 1 rnd even.

NEXT RND: (dec rnd) *K2tog, ssk; rep from * 3 more times—8 sts rem.

NEXT RND: [P1, k1] 4 times.

NEXT RND: (dec rnd) [K2tog] 4 times—4 sts rem.

Break yarn and draw through rem sts. Pull tight to gather and fasten off on WS.

Finishing

Buttonband

Pick up and knit 18 sts along one short edge of ribbed band.

ROW 1: (WS) *P2, k2; rep from * to last 2 sts, p2.

Work 2 more rows even in rib.

NEXT ROW: (RS; buttonhole row) K2, p1, p2tog, yo, k1, p2, k2, p2, k1, yo, p2tog, p1, k2.

NEXT ROW: *P2, k2; rep from * to last 2 sts, p2.

NEXT ROW: (RS; dec row) K2, p2tog, k2, p2, k2, p2, k2, p2tog, k2—16 sts rem.

NEXT ROW: P2, k1, p2, k2, p2, k2, p2, k1, p2.

NEXT ROW: (RS; dec row) K2, p2tog, k1, p2, k2, p2, k1, p2tog, k2—14 sts rem.

NEXT ROW: (WS; dec row) P2, k1, p1, k2tog, p2, k2tog, p1, k1, p2—12 sts rem.

With RS facing, BO all sts in patt. Weave in loose ends. Sew buttons to ribbed band opposite buttonholes.

Picking Up Stitches Evenly Along an Edge

When a pattern instructs you to pick up a specific number of stitches along an edge, save yourself some frustration with a simple trick. First, measure your piece, then gather locking stitch markers or safety pins. If you have only a small area, you may find that just dividing your piece into two sections will be enough. For longer edges, use more markers and divide your piece into four or more equal sections, using a ruler and placing locking markers at even intervals along the piece. Now divide the number of stitches that you need to pick up by the number of sections you've created and you'll have a much more manageable number to keep track of.

Transitions
hat & scarf

- -

by **Ruthie Nussbaum**

For this simple cabled hat-and-scarf set, Ruthie Nussbaum kept things interesting by working in gradational color stripes. She knitted with three strands of yarn throughout, but changed one strand at a time to create smooth gradations from dark to light (and back to dark for the scarf). The eight-stitch pattern repeat is easily memorized and the knitting goes quickly at a gauge of 4½ stitches to the inch.

Finished Size

HAT: 19" (48.5 cm) circumference and 7½" (19 cm) tall, after blocking. To fit an adult.

SCARF: About 4¼" (11 cm) wide and 72" (183 cm) long, after blocking.

Yarn

Fingering weight (#1 Super Fine).

SHOWN HERE: Dale of Norway Baby Ull (100% wool; 180 yd [164 m]/50 g): #4227 (burgundy; dark), #4018 (red; medium), #3718 (tomato red; light) 3 skeins each for both scarf and hat.

Needles

Size U.S. 9 (5.5 mm): straight or circular (cir) for scarf; 16" (40 cm) cir and set of 4 or 5 double-pointed (dpn) for hat.

Adjust needle size if necessary to obtain the correct gauge.

Notions

Cable needle (cn); tapestry needle; marker (m) for hat only.

Gauge

18 stitches and 25 rows = 4" (10 cm) in stockinette stitch with three strands of yarn.

STITCH GUIDE

Hat Pattern
(multiple of 7 sts)

RNDS 1, 5, AND 7: *K4, p3; rep from * to end of rnd.

RNDS 2, 4, AND 6: *K4, p1, yo, p2tog; rep from * to end of rnd.

RND 3: *Sl 2 sts onto cn and hold in back, k2, k2 from cn, p3; rep from * to end of rnd.

RND 8: Rep Rnd 2.

Repeat Rounds 1–8 for pattern.

Scarf Pattern
(multiple of 7 sts + 5)

ROWS 1, 5, AND 7: (RS) K1, p3, *k4, p3; rep from * to last st, k1.

ROWS 2, 4, AND 6: K2, yo, k2tog, *p4, k1, yo, k2tog; rep from * to last st, k1.

ROW 3: K1, p3, *sl 2 sts onto cn and hold in back, k2, k2 from cn, p3; rep from * to last st, k1.

ROW 8: Rep Row 2.

Repeat Rows 1–8 for pattern.

Hat

With three strands of the dark shade held tog and cir needle, CO 84 sts. Place marker (pm) and join for working in rnds, being careful not to twist sts. Rep Rnd 1 of hat patt (see Stitch Guide) 4 times for border—4 rnds total. Work Rnds 2–8 of patt, then rep Rnds 1–8 three more times, then work Rnds 1–3 once more and *at the same time* change colors as foll: Work with three strands dark for 2½" (6.5 cm), work with two strands dark and one strand medium for ½" (1.3 cm), work with one strand dark and two strands medium for ½" (1.3 cm), work with three strands medium for 1½" (3.8 cm), work with two strands medium and one strand light for ½" (1.3 cm), work with one strand medium and two strands light for ½" (1.3 cm)—piece measures about 6" (15 cm) from CO.

Shape Top

Work with three strands of light to end, dec as foll, changing to dpn when there are too few sts to fit comfortably around cir needle:

RND 1: K4, p2tog, *p1, k4, p2tog; rep from * to last st, p1—72 sts rem.

RNDS 2, 4, and 6: Knit.

RND 3: *K4, p2tog; rep from * to end of rnd—60 sts rem.

RND 5: *K3, p2tog; rep from * to end of rnd—48 sts rem.

RND 7: *K2, p2tog; rep from * across round—36 sts rem.

RND 8: *K1, p2tog; rep from * to end of rnd—24 sts rem.

RND 9: *K2tog; rep from * to end of rnd—12 sts rem.

RND 10: *K2tog; rep from * to end of rnd—6 sts rem.

Cut yarn, leaving an 8" (20.5 cm) tail. Thread tail on tapestry needle and run through rem sts 2 times, pull tight to gather sts, and fasten off to WS of hat.

Weave in loose ends. Block lightly.

Scarf

With three strands of the dark shade held tog, CO 26 sts. Work in scarf patt (see Stitch Guide) and *at the same time* change colors as foll: Work with three strands dark yarn for 8" (20.5 cm), work with two strands dark and one strand medium for 3" (7.5 cm), work with one strand dark and two strands medium for 4" (10 cm), work with three strands medium for 6" (15 cm), work with two strands medium and one strand light for 2" (5 cm), work with one strand medium and two strands light for 4" (10 cm), work with three strands light for 10" (25.5 cm), work with two strands light and one strand medium for 4" (10 cm), work with one strand light and two strands medium for 2" (5 cm), work with three strands medium for 6" (15 cm), work with two strands medium and one strand dark for 4" (10 cm), work with one strand medium and two strands dark for 3" (7.5 cm), work with three strands dark for 8" (20.5 cm), ending with Row 4 of patt. BO all sts.

Weave in loose ends. Block lightly to finished measurements.

Toe-up
travelers

- -

by **Ann Budd**

These socks begin with a traveling-stitch "wing" pattern found in a Japanese book of stitch patterns called *Knitting Patterns Book 250*. The socks are worked from the toe up and another pattern is added at the sides of the leg to bring the stitch count to an appropriate number for a leg circumference. A short-row heel minimizes design interruption at the heel, and for the cuff, the wrapped-stitch pattern continues up the sides of the leg but the traveling stitches cease in the wings pattern. A tiny cable pattern runs up the center of the motif and a stretchy sewn bind-off forms an elastic edge at the cuff.

Finished Size
About 7½" (19 cm) foot circumference, 10" (25.5 cm) foot length from back of heel to tip of toe, and 8½" (21.5 cm) leg length from top of cuff to base of heel.

Yarn
Fingering weight (#1 Super Fine).

SHOWN HERE: Quince & Company Tern (75% wool, 25% silk; 226 yd [206 m]/50 g): #750 kelp, 2 skeins.

Needles
FOOT AND LOWER LEG: size U.S. 1 (2.25 mm): set of 5 double-pointed (dpn).

UPPER LEG: size U.S. 2 (2.75 mm): set of 5 dpn.

Adjust needle size if necessary to obtain the correct gauge.

Notions
Markers (m); cable needle (optional); tapestry needle.

Gauge
18 sts and 26 rnds = 2" (5 cm) in St st on smaller needles, worked in rnds.

40 sts of Wings Instep chart measures 3" (7.5 cm) wide on smaller needles.

Notes

- *The twisted stitches are easiest to work using needles that have long sharp tips.*

- *To lengthen the foot, work the desired number of additional rounds of stockinette stitch after reaching the total number of foot stitches but before beginning the charted pattern.*

- *To increase the foot circumference, work more toe increases, then distribute the extra stitches evenly between the instep and sole. Work the instep stitches in the purl columns on each side of the main motif (between the wings and the wrapped stitches) where they will cause the least disruption. Work the extra sole stitches in stockinette stitch. When working the first half of the heel, repeat the required rows until a right-side row of "paired sts, k14" has been worked, then work the second half as written. Distribute the extra stitches on the back of the leg in the purl columns flanking the wings pattern, just as for the instep (which continues along the front of the leg).*

STITCH GUIDE

4-St Wrap

Insert right needle between the 4th and 5th sts on left needle, draw up a loop and place it on left needle, knit the new loop tog with the st after it, then k2, k1tbl.

Ssp

Slip 2 sts individually kwise, return these 2 sts to left needle tip, then purl them tog through their back loops—1 st dec'd.

Sssp

Slip 3 sts individually kwise, return these 3 sts to left needle tip, then purl them tog through their back loops—2 sts dec'd.

Toe

With two smaller dpn held tog and using the Turkish/Eastern method (page 89), CO 8 sts. Divide sts on 3 dpn so that there are 2 sole sts on Needle 1, 4 instep sts on Needle 2, and 2 sole sts on Needle 3; rnd begins at center of sole (between Needles 1 and 3).

INC RND: On Needle 1, knit to last st, M1 (see Glossary), k1; on Needle 2, k1, M1, knit to last st, M1, k1; on Needle 3, k1, M1, knit to end—4 sts inc'd.

Rep the inc rnd on the next 7 rnds—40 sts. Rep the inc rnd every other rnd 10 times—80 sts; 20 sole sts on Needle 1, 40 instep sts on Needle 2, and 20 sole sts on Needle 3.

Foot

Working the sole sts in St st as established, work 40 instep sts (Needle 2) in patt from Wings Instep chart (page 91) until Rnds 1–24 of chart have been worked 3 times, ending at the end of instep sts (Needle 2) on Rnd 24 of chart (leave sts of Needle 3 unworked)—72 chart rnds completed; piece measures about 8" (20.5 cm) from tip of toe (see Notes for adding length).

Turkish/Eastern Cast-On

This method is worked by first wrapping the yarn around two parallel needles, then using a third needle to knit the loops on each of the two needles. The loops on one needle are the foundation for the instep and the loops on the other needle are the foundation for the sole.

Hold two double-pointed needles parallel to each other. Leaving a 4" (10 cm) tail hanging to the front between the two needles, wrap the yarn around both needles from back to front half the number of times as desired stitches (four wraps shown here for 8 stitches total), then bring the yarn forward between the needles (**Figure 1**).

Use a third needle to knit across the loops on the top needle, keeping the third needle on top of both the other needles when knitting the first stitch (**Figure 2**).

With the right side facing, rotate the two cast-on needles like the hands of a clock so that the bottom needle is on the top (**Figure 3**).

Knit across the loops on the new top needle (**Figure 4**).

Rotate the needles again and use a third needle to knit the first 2 stitches of the new top needle. There will now be 2 stitches each on two needles and 4 stitches on another needle (**Figure 5**).

The two needles with 2 stitches each will form the bottom of the foot; the needle with 4 stitches will form the top of the foot. Using a fourth needle, begin working in rounds.

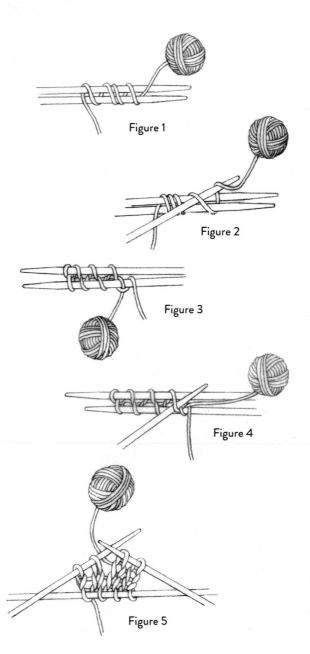

Figure 1

Figure 2

Figure 3

Figure 4

Figure 5

Heel

Arrange sts so that all 40 sole sts (Needle 1 and Needle 3) are on the same needle for the heel and divide the 40 instep sts on 2 needles to work later. Work the 40 sole stitches back and forth in short-rows in two halves as foll.

First Half

Work 1 less st each short-row as foll:

ROW 1: (RS) K39, turn work—1 regular st unworked at end of needle.

ROW 2: (WS) Bring yarn from back to front over right needle to create a backward yo, p38, leaving last st unworked, turn—1 regular st unworked at end of row; 1 regular st and 1 "paired st" consisting of a stitch plus a yo at beg of row.

ROW 3: Bring yarn from front to back over right needle to create a normal yo, knit to paired st at end of row, turn—1 paired st and 1 regular st unworked at each end of row.

ROW 4: Bring yarn from back to front over right needle to create a backward yo, purl to paired st at end of row, turn.

ROW 5: Bring yarn from front to back over right needle to create a normal yo, knit to paired st at end of row, turn.

Rep Rows 4 and 5 ten more times, adding another paired st at the end of each row and ending with a RS row—12 paired sts and 1 regular st unworked at each side. Last row completed was worked as "yo, k1 (to form the 12th st/yo pair), k14."

Second Half

Work 1 more st each short-row as foll:

ROW 1: (RS) Cont with the same RS row, k1 (the knit st of the paired st), correct the mount of the yo so

that its leading leg is in front of the needle, k2tog (the yo tog with the knit st of the foll paired st), turn work, leaving rem yo of the pair unworked.

ROW 2: (WS) Bring yarn from back to front over right needle to create a backward yo, purl to the first paired st, p1 (the purl st of the pair), ssp (the yo of the pair tog with the purl st of the foll pair; see Stitch Guide), turn, leaving rem yo of pair unworked.

ROW 3: Bring yarn from front to back over right needle to create a normal yo, knit to the first paired st, k1 (the knit st of the pair), correct the mount of the next 2 yo's, k3tog (the 2 yo's tog with the knit st of the foll pair), turn, leaving rem yo of the pair unworked.

ROW 4: Bring yarn from back to front over right needle to create a backward yo, purl to the first paired st, p1 (the purl st of the pair), sssp (the 2 yo's tog with the purl st of the foll pair; see Stitch Guide), turn, leaving rem yo of pair unworked.

Rep Rows 3 and 4 until all heel sts have been worked, ending with a WS row—there will be 41 sts on the needle; 40 regular sts and 1 yo paired with the last st on the needle (when viewed from the RS).

Joining Round

With RS facing, bring yarn from front to back to create a normal yo, knit to the paired st at the end of the needle, k1 (the knit st of the pair), transfer the yo to the beg of the instep sts and work it tog with the first instep st as p2tog (counts as the first st from Rnd 1 of Wings Instep chart), work the next 38 sts according to the chart, transfer the yo at the beg of the heel sts to the end of the instep needle and work it tog with the last instep st as ssp (counts as last st from Rnd 1 of chart), then work the first 29 sts from Rnd 1 of Wings Instep chart again over the first 29 heel sts, leaving rem 11 heel sts unworked—80 sts total.

Wings Instep

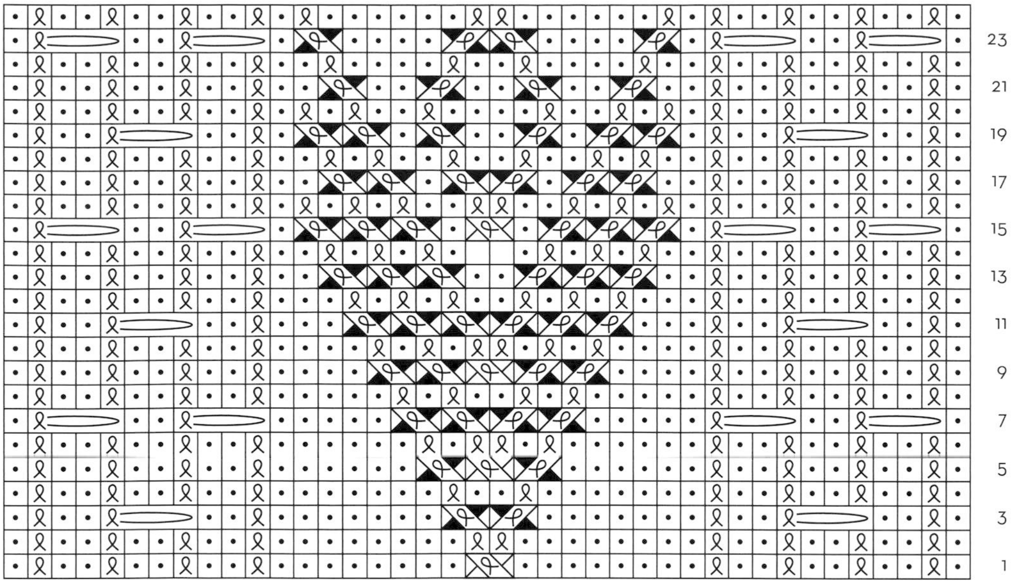

- knit
- k1tbl
- purl
- 4-st wrap (see Stitch Guide)
- sl 1 st onto cn and hold in front, k1tbl, k1tbl from cn
- sl 1 st onto cn and hold in back, k1tbl, p1 from cn
- sl 1 st onto cn and hold in front, p1, k1tbl from cn

tip Traditionally, cuffs are worked in some type of rib pattern. If possible, a ribbed cuff is best integrated with the leg if the knit or purl stitches in the cuff flow uninterrupted into the knit or purl stitches in the leg pattern.

Wings Leg

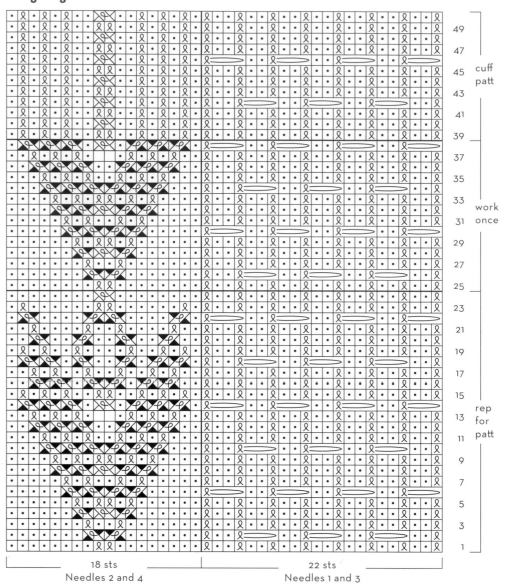

18 sts
Needles 2 and 4

22 sts
Needles 1 and 3

cuff patt

work once

rep for patt

Leg

Rearrange sts on 4 dpn as foll: Place 11 rem unworked sts and next 11 sts on Needle 1 for 22 sts in wrapped-st patt at side of leg, place next 18 sts on Needle 2 for main motif at front of leg, place next 22 sts on Needle 3 for wrapped-st patt at other side of leg, and place rem 18 sts on Needle 4 for main motif at back of leg. Rnd begs at start of Needle 1 with 22 sts in wrapped-st patt. Work Rnds 1–24 of Wings Leg chart once, then work Rnds 1–14 once more—piece measures about 5½" (14 cm) from base of heel. Change to larger dpn and work Rnds 15–38 once—piece measures about 7½" (19 cm) from base of heel. Work Rnds 39–50 for cuff—12 cuff rnds total; piece measures about 8½" (21.5 cm) from base of heel.

Finishing

Cut yarn, leaving a 26" (66 cm) tail. Thread tail on a tapestry needle and use the sewn method (see page 121) to BO all sts.

Weave in loose ends. Block to measurements.

Grand Army Plaza
shawl

- -

by **Melissa Wehrle**

A full circular shawl is very pretty and impressive laid out flat in its full glory, but you only get half the effect when it's worn.

Enter the half-circle shawl! You can wear this the same way you would a triangle or full circle, but all your knitting will be seen and appreciated. As an added bonus, the garter-based lace patterns used here are mostly reversible, and the fabric doesn't curl.

This shawl evokes the tucked-away niches of green that you can find anywhere in New York City.

Finished Size

About 54" (137 cm) across top edge and 24" (61 cm) long from center of top edge to lower point, blocked.

Yarn

Laceweight (#0 Lace).

SHOWN HERE: Sundara Yarn *Silk Lace* (100% silk; 1000 yd [914 m]/100 g): island breeze, 1 skein.

Needles

Size U.S. 4 (3.5 mm). 24" (61 cm) cir needle and one double-pointed needle (dpn).

Adjust needle size, if necessary, to obtain the correct gauge; exact gauge is not critical for this project.

Notions

Tapestry needle; rustproof blocking pins.

Gauge

16 sts and 24 rows = 4" (10 cm) in average gauge of lace patts, after blocking.

Notes

- *The shawl begins in the center of the upper edge and is worked downward with increases to shape the half circle.*

- *The lace edging is worked perpendicular to the body of the shawl, joining one edging stitch together with one live shawl stitch at the end of every even-numbered edging row until all the shawl stitches have been consumed.*

STITCH GUIDE

Roman Stripe

(worked on an even number of patt sts + 4 edge sts)

ROW 1: K2 (edge sts), *yo, k1; rep from * to last 2 sts, k2 (edge sts)—sts have inc'd to twice the original patt sts, plus 2 edge sts at each side.

ROW 2: K2, purl to last 2 sts, k2.

ROW 3: K2, *k2tog; rep from * to last 2 sts, k2—sts have dec'd to original number.

ROWS 4 AND 5: K2, *yo, k2tog; rep from to last 2 sts, k2.

ROWS 6 and 7: Knit.

Rep Rows 1-7 for patt.

Madeira Mesh

(multiple of 6 sts + 7)

ROWS 1-6: K2, *yo, p3tog, yo, k3; rep from *, to last 5 sts, yo, p3tog, yo, k2.

ROWS 7-12: K2, *k3, yo, p3tog, yo; rep from * to last 5 sts, k5.

Rep Rows 1-12 for patt.

Double Fagotting

(multiple of 4 sts + 1)

ROW 1: (RS) K3, *yo, p3tog, yo, k1; rep from * to last 2 sts, k2.

ROW 2: (WS) K2, p2tog, yo, k1, *yo, p3tog, yo, k1; rep from * last 4 sts, yo, p2tog, k2.

Rep Rows 1 and 2 for patt.

Shawl

CO 8 sts.

ROW 1: Knit.

ROW 2: K2, *yo, k1; rep from * to last 2 sts, k2—12 sts.

ROWS 3-5: Knit.

ROW 6: K2, *yo, k1; rep from * to last 2 sts, k2—20 sts.

ROWS 7-12: Knit.

ROW 13: K2, *yo, k1; rep from * to last 2 sts, k2—36 sts.

ROWS 14-25: Knit.

ROW 26: K2, *yo, k1; rep from * to last 2 sts, k2—68 sts.

ROWS 27-28: Knit.

ROWS 29-49: Work Rows 1-7 of Roman Stripe patt (see Stitch Guide) 3 times.

ROWS 50-51: Knit.

ROW 52: K2, *yo, k1; rep from * to last 2 sts, k2—132 sts.

ROWS 53-58: Knit.

ROW 59: K2, M1 (see Glossary), knit to end—133 sts.

ROWS 60-101: Work Rows 1-12 of Madeira Mesh patt (see Stitch Guide) 3 times, then work Rows 1-6 once more.

ROW 102: K2, *yo, k1; rep from * to last 3 sts, k3—261 sts.

ROWS 103-142: Work Rows 1 and 2 of Double Fagotting patt (see Stitch Guide) 20 times.

ROWS 143-145: Knit.

Lace Edging

Turn the work so the end of the cir needle with working yarn is in your right hand. Use the backward-loop method (see Glossary) to CO 10 sts onto the end of the right needle—271 sts total; 261 live shawl sts, 10 edging sts. Turn the work so the end of the cir needle with the new CO sts is in your left hand and use the dpn instead of the other cir needle tip to work the edging as foll:

SETUP ROW: K9, k2tog (last edging st tog with shawl st after it), turn work—10 edging sts; 1 shawl st joined.

ROW 1: K2, yo, k2tog, k2, k2tog, yo, k2.

ROW 2: K3, yo, k2, yo, k4, k2tog (last edging st tog with next shawl st), turn work—12 edging sts; 1 shawl st joined.

ROW 3: K2, yo, k10—13 edging sts.

ROW 4: BO 3 sts (1 st rem on right needle after last BO), k8, k2tog (last edging st tog with next shawl st), turn work—10 edging sts; 1 shawl st joined.

Rep Rows 1-4 (do not rep the setup row) 129 more times—10 edging sts rem; all shawl sts have been joined. BO rem sts.

Finishing

Weave in all loose ends. Soak shawl in a basin of water. To block, pin the top edge along a straight line to about 54" (137 cm) wide. Pin the center point straight down from the middle of the top edging to measure about 24" (61 cm) long, then pin out the rem points on each side of center, forming a half-circle shape.

Sideways
grande hat

- -

by **Laura Irwin**

Welcome the bitterest winters in this oversize hat. This ribbed cloche-shaped cap, worked in warm alpaca, is finished with a twisted faux cable that runs from brim to crown. Wear the cable off center or at the side of the head.

Finished Size
20" (51 cm) circumference. To fit 21½–23" (54.5–58.5 cm) head circumference.

Yarn
Chunky weight (Bulky #5).

SHOWN HERE: Plymouth Baby Alpaca Grande (100% baby alpaca; 110 yd [101 m]/100 g): #401 gray, 2 skeins.

Needles
U.S. size 7 (4.5 mm), U.S. size 8 (5 mm), U.S. size 9 (5.5 mm), and U.S. size 10 (6 mm).

Adjust needle size if necessary to obtain the correct gauge.

Notions
2 locking-ring markers; tapestry needle.

Gauge
22½ sts and 20 rows = 4" (10 cm) in rib patt on largest needles.

Construction
The hat is knitted from side to side in one piece, then stitches are picked up for the crown and cable.

Hat

Brim

With largest needles, CO 42 sts.

ROW 1: (WS) *K2, p1; rep from * to last 3 sts, k3.

ROW 2: Work sts as they appear.

Rep Rows 1 and 2 until piece measures 14½" (37 cm) from CO.

Change to second largest needles and continue in patt until piece measures 16" (40.5 cm) from CO.

Change to second smallest needles and continue in patt until piece measures 17½" (44.5 cm) from CO.

Change to smallest needles and continue in patt until piece measures 20" (51 cm) from CO.

BO all sts in patt.

Crown

With second largest needles, RS facing, and beg at CO edge, pick up and knit 68 sts along selvedge to BO edge.

ROWS 1, 3, 5, 7, AND 9: (WS) Purl.

ROW 2: (dec row) K1, *k4, k2tog; rep from * to last st, k1—57 sts rem.

ROW 4: K1, *k3, k2tog; rep from * to last st, k1—46 sts rem.

ROW 6: K1, *k2, k2tog; rep from * to last st, k1—35 sts rem.

ROW 8: K1, *k1, k2tog; rep from * to last st, k1—24 sts rem.

ROW 10: K1, *k2tog; rep from * to last st, k1—13 sts rem.

ROW 11: P1, *p2tog; rep from * to last 2 sts, p2—8 sts rem.

Cut yarn, leaving an 8" (20.5 cm) tail. Pull tail through rem 8 sts and fasten off inside.

With yarn threaded on a tapestry needle, use mattress st (see

Running Stitch

Holding the pieces to be joined together, pass a threaded needle from WS to RS and back, creating stitches that look like a small dashed line of equal lengths

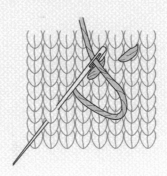

Glossary) to sew side of hat, being sure to line up ribs.

Cable

First Strap

At bottom edge of hat, measure 1" (2.5 cm) on each side of seam. Mark with locking-ring markers.

With WS facing and largest needles, pick up and knit 4 sts between m and seam on each side of m—8 sts total.

ROW 1: (RS of hat; WS of strap) K2, p1, k2, p1, k2.

ROW 2: P2, k1, p2, k1, p2.

Rep Rows 1 and 2 until piece measures 7¼" (18.5 cm) from picked up edge, ending with Row 1.

NEXT ROW: (bind-off row) P1, p2tog, pass purl st over p2tog to BO 1 st, BO all sts to last 3 sts, p2tog, pass st over p2tog to BO 1 st, p1, pass p2tog over purl st to BO 1 st. Fasten off last st—no sts rem.

Second Strap

With WS facing, measure 2" (5 cm) to the right of first cable strap and mark with locking-ring marker. With WS facing and largest needles, pick up and knit 8 sts between marker and first strap.

Beg with Row 1, work as for first strap.

Finishing

Wrap the two straps around each other 3 times, being sure that they lie flat against hat. With yarn threaded on a tapestry needle, sew BO edges of straps to last horizontal rib of hat near crown. Use running st to secure cable to hat. Weave in loose ends.

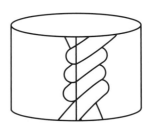

Construction Diagram

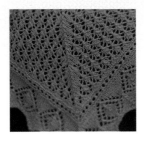

Ene's
scarf

by **Nancy Bush**

Nancy Bush named her scarf in honor of her Estonian friend Ene Sokk. Nancy's triangular scarf is based on traditional shawls from the seaside town of Haapsalu where local women have been knitting lace garments from sheep's wool since the early nineteenth century.

The shawl is worked by casting on for the two sides and worked to the center of the top edge. Four decreases are made on every decrease row; two are made just inside the border on the outer edges of the triangle, and a double decrease is worked along the center axis.

Finished Size
About 32" (81.5 cm) from bottom of point to top edge, measured straight up the center, 56" (142 cm) across the top edge, and 40" (101.5 cm) from bottom of point to top edge, measured along the side, before blocking.

Yarn
Blackberry Ridge Lace Weight Silk Blend (75% wool, 25% silk; 350 yd [320 m]/2 oz [57] g): willow, 2 skeins.

Needles
Size 6 (4 mm): 32" (80-cm) or longer circular (cir).

Adjust needle size if necessary to obtain the correct gauge.

Notions
Markers (m); tapestry needle; coilless safety pin or removable marker; 2 double-pointed needles (dpn) the same size or smaller than the main needles for working three-needle bind-off.

Gauge
11 sts and 18 rows = 2" (5 cm) in St st.

Notes

- *This scarf is cast on along the lower two sides and then decreased as it is worked upwards to the center of the top edge.*

- *The sections of the scarf inside the border markers have four decreases on every RS row (one decrease inside each border marker, and a double decrease centered in the middle of the scarf). Rows 23, 27, and 31 of Chart 2 are exceptions to this rule, and have six decreases each. Rows 23 and 31 have an extra single decrease just inside each border, and Row 27 has an extra k2tog on either side of center that is not paired with a yarnover. Row 179 of Chart 4 has only the centered double decrease.*

- *If desired, you may change to a shorter circular needle (optional) as the number of stitches decreases.*

Scarf

With two strands of yarn held tog, and using the knitted method (see Glossary), CO 375 sts. Drop one of the strands and cont using a single strand of yarn throughout. Work Rows 1–22 from right and left halves of Chart 1, placing markers (pm) for the borders as indicated, and placing a coilless pin or removable stitch marker in the center st (move this pin up as the work progresses).

note: *The center section of the scarf will dec by 4 sts every RS row, each border section will inc 1 st every other row four times, until there are eight border sts at each side. There will be 339 sts when Row 22 of Chart 1 has been completed.*

Change to Chart 2 and work Rows 23 to 32—313 sts. Change to Chart 3 and work Rows 33 to 56 once—265 sts. For Rows 57 to 152, rep Rows 33 to 56 four more times—73 sts rem. Change to Chart 4 and work Rows 153 to 179 once—19 sts rem (the center st and 9 sts at each side). Work the next WS row as foll: K2tog, yo, k7, k2tog, k8—18

sts rem. Arrange sts 9 each on two dpn and hold with RS tog. With the main needle and using the three-needle method (see Glossary), BO the two groups of sts tog.

Finishing

Pin scarf out to desired shape, taking care to pin out the points along the CO edge. Place a damp towel over the scarf to block. When dry, weave in loose ends.

Chart 1

Legend:
- k on RS; p on WS
- p on RS; k on WS
- yo
- k2tog on both RS and WS
- sl 1 as if to knit, k1, pass slipped st over
- sl 1 as if to knit, k2tog, pass slipped st over
- no stitch
- pattern repeat
- marker position

Row numbers: 21, 19, 17, 15, 13, 11, 9, 7, 5, 3, 1

rep 11 times

center st

rep 11 times

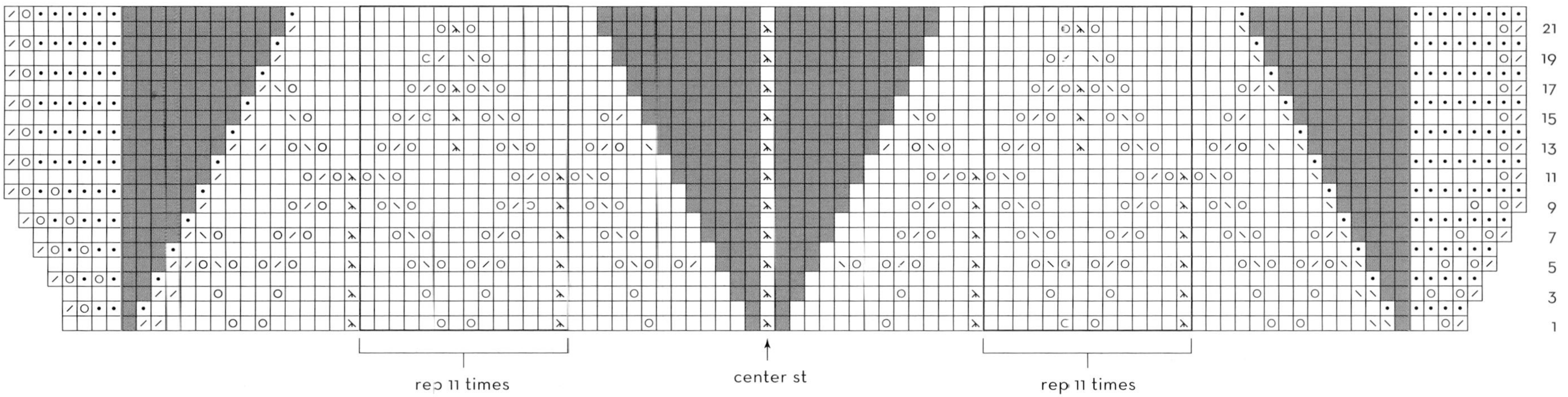

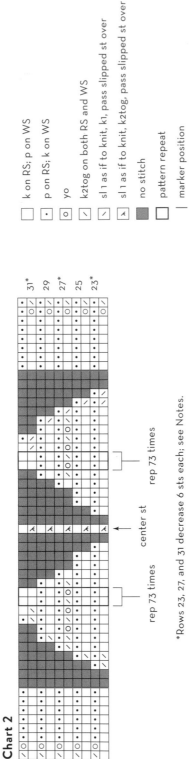

Legend:

- ☐ k on RS; p on WS
- · p on RS; k on WS
- ○ yo
- ╲ k2tog on both RS and WS
- ╱ sl 1 as if to knit, k1, pass slipped st over
- ⋏ sl 1 as if to knit, k2tog, pass slipped st over
- ▨ no stitch
- ☐ pattern repeat
- │ marker position

Chart 2

31*
29
27*
25
23*

rep 73 times

center st

rep 73 times

*Rows 23, 27, and 31 decrease 6 sts each; see Notes.

Chart 3

55
53
51
49
47
45
43
41
39
37
35
33

center st

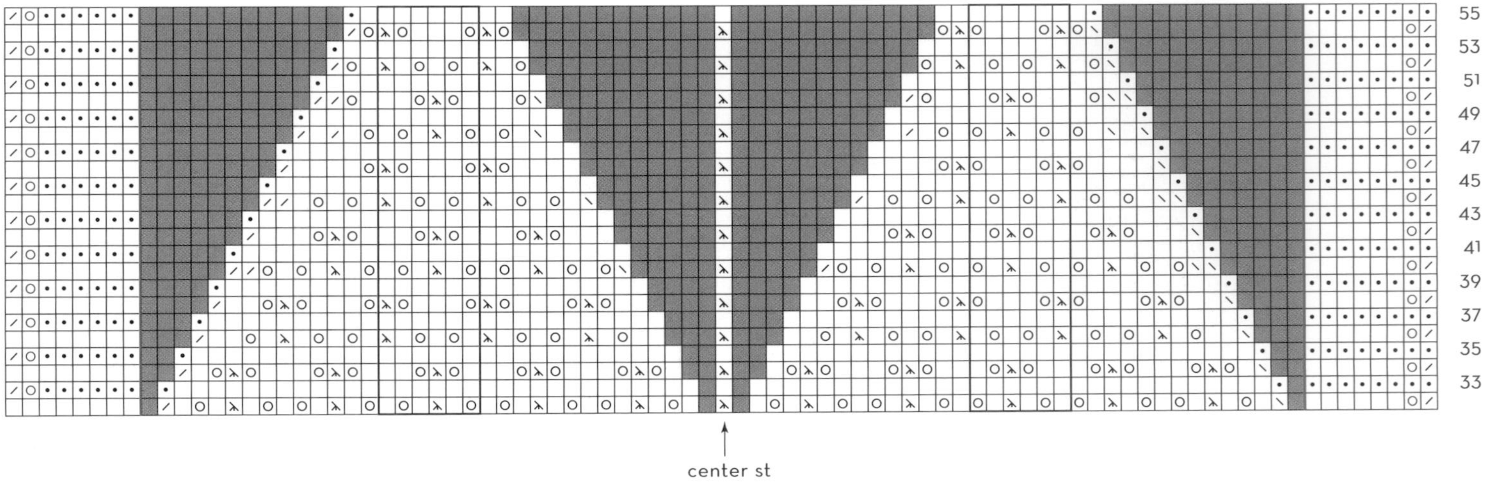

Chart 4

179 177 175 173 171 169 167 165 163 161 159 157 155 153

← center st

Lily of the Valley
shawl

by **Nancy Bush**

Some of the most beautiful lace patterns come from Eastern Europe. The lily of the valley pattern used in this shawl is a traditional but enduringly popular motif that originated in Estonia. The shawl is worked as a large rectangle with sprigs of lily of the valley accented with the characteristic nupps (buds or buttons) that alternate with sprigs without nupps. Every other row is purled to produce a smooth stockinette-stitch background that doesn't interfere with the lace pattern. The edging, however, is worked with a garter stitch background in rounds that grow outward from the edges of the rectangle and end with sharp points along the bind-off edge.

Finished Size
About 23" (58.5 cm) wide and 60" (152.5 cm) long.

Yarn
Lace weight (no CYCA equivalent).

SHOWN HERE: Jaggerspun Superfine Merino (100% merino; 630 yd [576 m]/2 oz): mushroom (pale grayish taupe), 2 skeins.

Needles
Size 6 (4 mm): straight and 32" (80 cm) circular (cir).

Adjust needle size if necessary to obtain the correct gauge.

Notions
Several yards of sport- or worsted-weight cotton in contrasting color for provisional cast-on; markers (m; 1 in a color or style different from the others); size G/6 (4 mm) crochet hook; tapestry needle.

Gauge
24 sts and 30 rnds = 4" (10 cm) in stockinette stitch worked in the round before blocking.

STITCH GUIDE

Nupp

Working very loosely, work [k1, yo, k1, yo, k1] all in same st—5 nupp sts made from 1 st. On the foll row, purl these 5 sts tog to dec to 1 st.

Note: The initial nupp sts must be worked more loosely than customary in order to work them as p5tog on the next row.

Center Rectangle

With crochet hook and contrasting yarn, make a crochet chain (see Glossary) about 110 loops long. Cut yarn, pull the tail through the last chain loop, and tie a knot or loop in this tail so you can find it later when you want to remove the cast-on. With main yarn and using the crochet chain provisional technique (see Glossary), pick up and knit 100 sts in the back loop "bumps" on the underside of the crochet chain, beg and ending 5 ch sts from each end.

ROW 1: (WS) K1 (edge st), k3 (garter "frame" sts), place marker (pm), k92, pm, k3 (garter frame sts), k1 (edge st).

ROW 2: (RS) Sl 1 pwise with yarn in front (wyf), bring yarn to back, knit to end of row.

ROW 3: Sl 1 pwise wyf (edge st), bring yarn to back, knit to last st, k1tbl (edge st).

ROWS 4–7: Rep Row 3 four more times, ending with a WS row—4 garter st ridges completed.

Change to Lily of the Valley chart, and work in patt from chart until Rows 1–28 have been repeated 10

Lily Chart

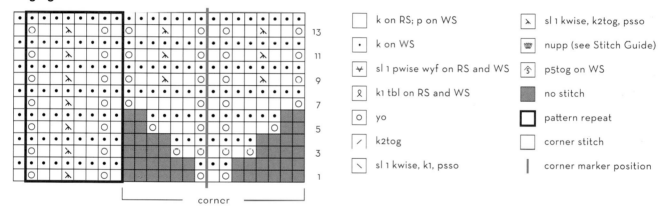

Edging

corner

Legend		Legend
☐ k on RS; p on WS		⋏ sl 1 kwise, k2tog, psso
• k on WS		⊎ nupp (see Stitch Guide)
¥ sl 1 pwise wyf on RS and WS		⑤ p5tog on WS
Q k1 tbl on RS and WS		▨ no stitch
O yo		☐ pattern repeat
╱ k2tog		☐ corner stitch
╲ sl 1 kwise, k1, psso		┃ corner marker position

times, then work Rows 1–14 once more—294 patt rows total.

NEXT ROW: (RS) Sl 1 pwise wyf, knit to last st, k1tbl. Rep the last row 7 more times—4 garter ridges completed. Do not cut yarn.

Edging

note: *Pick up sts for edging along the chained selvedges as foll: Pick up 1 st in the first selvedge chain st by inserting the needle tip under both legs of the st, pick up 1 st in the back half of the second chain by inserting the needle tip under only the back leg of that chain, then pick up 1 st from the same whole chain by inserting the needle tip under both legs—3 sts picked up from 2 chain selvedge sts.*

Change to cir needle. K1 (corner st), place different-color marker to indicate beg of rnd, knit to end, inc 14 sts evenly spaced and removing other markers as you come them—114 sts. With the RS of piece still facing, pick up and knit 234 sts along one long side, pm after the first picked-up st (corner st)—348 sts total; if you have made any length adjustments, make sure the number of sts picked up along the selvedge is a multiple of 8 plus 2. Carefully undo the marked end of the crochet chain, pull gently to unzip, and place live sts on needle as they become free—100 sts released from CO edge. Knit the first freed st (corner st), pm, knit to end inc 14 sts evenly spaced—462 sts. Pick up and knit 234 sts along rem long side, pm after the first picked up st (corner st)—696 sts; 4 corner sts, each with a marker immediately after it; first corner st of rnd marked with a different color;

if you have made length adjustments, be sure to pick up the same number of sts as for the other side. Work Rnd 1 of Edging chart as foll: *On the first short side, k1 (corner st), slip marker (sl m), yo, [k1, yo, k2, sl 1 kwise, k2tog, psso, k2, yo] 14 times, k1, yo (shown as first st on chart, before center st). On the first long side, k1 (corner st), sl m, yo, [k1, yo, k2, sl 1 kwise, k2tog, psso, k2, yo] 29 times, k1, yo (first st of chart). Rep from * for the rem short and long sides to complete Rnd 1 of chart—2 sts inc'd at each corner; 8 sts inc'd total. For Rnd 2 of chart, purl all sts. Cont until Rnd 14 of chart has been completed—752 sts. Join a second strand of yarn, and BO with 2 strands held tog as foll: Sl 1 pwise, *k1, insert left needle tip into front of these 2 sts from left to right and knit them tog; rep from * until last 2 sts have been knitted tog, cut yarn, and pull through last st to fasten off.

Finishing

Block shawl to about 28" (71 cm) wide and 66" (167.5 cm) long by pinning the damp shawl on a towel; piece will relax to about 23" (58.5 cm) wide and 60" (152.5 cm) long when unpinned. Start by stretching each corner to the blocking measurements, then work from side to side, pinning out the "points" at the top of the [yo, k1, yo] columns of the edging. Allow to completely air-dry before removing pins. Weave in loose ends.

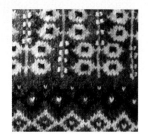

Märta
embroidered bag

- -

by **Lucinda Guy**

Inspired by the vibrant work of Märta Måås-Fjetterstöm, one of Sweden's foremost textile artists and pupil of Lilli Zickerman, who founded the Swedish Handicraft Association, the Märta bag is a lovely example of a well-designed, useful everyday object that is not only beautiful to look at but is beautiful to use.

Knitted in the round, the Märta bag is embroidered with simple cross-stitches, French knots, and duplicate-stitch details before being handwashed and slightly felted.

Finished Size
About 14¾" (37.5 cm) wide at base and 12" (30.5 cm) high, not including handles.

Yarn
Sportweight (#2 Fine).

SHOWN HERE: Ullcentrum Öland 2-Thread Wool Yarn (100% wool; 328 yd [300 m]/100 g): petrol (teal; A), red (B), cream (C), 1 skein each; yellow (D), small amount.

Note. This yarn has been discontinued. Please substitute any sportweight wool yarn that knits to gauge such as Brown Sheep Nature Spun Sport (100% wool; 184 yds [168 m]/50 g) Always remember to check your gauge when substituting yarns.

Needles
Size 3 mm (no exact U.S. equivalent; between U.S. size 2 and 3): 24" (60 cm) circular (cir).

Adjust needle size if necessary to obtain the correct gauge.

Notions
Tapestry needle; stitch holder (optional); ½ yd [0.5 m] of 36" (91.5 cm) or wider linen fabric for lining; sharp-point sewing needle and thread; one pair wooden purse handles with 10" to 11" (25.5 to 28 cm) wide slots.

Gauge
27 stitches and 29½ rounds = 4" (10 cm) in charted color patterns, worked in rounds.

Bag

With A, CO 200 sts. Place marker (pm) and join for working in rnds, being careful not to twist sts; rnd begins at side of bag where color changes between rnds will be less obvious. With A, knit 1 rnd. Work Rnds 1–27 of Diamonds chart. With A, knit 1 rnd.

DEC RND: With A, *k1, ssk, k97; rep from * once more—198 sts rem.

Work Rnds 1–39 of Hearts and Flowers chart. With A, knit 5 rnds— piece measures 10" (25.5 cm) from CO. Place last 99 sts of rnd on holder (optional) for one side of bag or allow sts to rest on cable portion of cir needle while working the other side. Work the first 99 sts of rnd back and forth in rows with A as foll:

ROW 1: (RS) K1, ssk, knit to last 3 sts, ssk, k1—2 sts dec'd.

ROW 2: (WS) Purl.

Rep Rows 1 and 2 ten more times—77 sts rem; piece measures 13" (33 cm) from CO. BO these 77 sts. Return 99 held sts to cir needle if they are not already on the needle and rejoin A with RS facing. Rep Rows 1 and 2 a total of 11 times—77 sts rem. BO all sts.

Finishing

Work embroidery (see page 118 for embroidery stitches) as indicated on charts as foll: With cream and yellow, work single duplicate stitches as shown on Diamonds chart. With red, work a small cross-stitch in the center of each small flower of Hearts and Flowers chart. In the middle of each large flower at the top of Hearts and Flowers chart, work a large cross-stitch with a vertical straight stitch at its center using yellow. Work French knots with teal, red, and yellow as

shown in Hearts and Flowers chart. Weave in loose ends.

Wash bag in warm soapy water, gently roll in a towel to squeeze out excess water, pull gently into shape, and allow to dry flat. When dry, press carefully with a warm iron over a damp cloth.

Lining

Using the knitted bag as a template, cut two pieces of linen lining fabric with a ½" (1.3 cm) seam allowance all the way around each piece. Sew lining pieces tog at the sides and across the bottom using sewing machine or sharp-point sewing needle, leaving the top 3" (7.5 cm) of each side unsewn. Press seams. Turn raw edges ½" (1.3 cm) to WS along upper part of lining and press. Turn lining WS

out and place lining inside bag so wrong sides of bag and lining are touching. With sewing needle and thread, slip-stitch lining to bag along the shaped top selvedges and across the BO edges. Insert the BO edge of one side into the slot of one handle, fold upper edge of bag 1" (2.5 cm) to WS, and sew securely in place with sewing needle and thread. Rep for other handle.

Hearts and Flowers

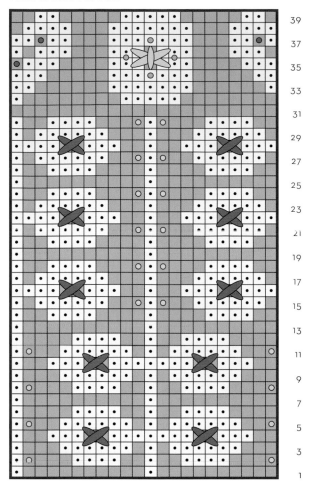

39
37
35
33
31
29
27
25
23
21
19
17
15
13
11
9
7
5
3
1

Diamonds

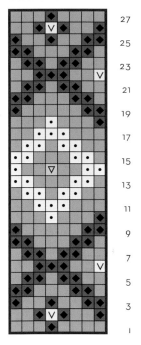

27
25
23
21
19
17
15
13
11
9
7
5
3
1

	A
	B
	C
V	knit with A, duplicate st with C
▽	knit with A, duplicate st with D
●	k with A, French knot with B
○	k with A, French knot with D
●	k with C, French knot with A
□	pattern repeat
✖	small cross-stitch with B
✳	large cross-stitch and vertical straight stitch with D

Embroidery Stitches

CROSS-STITCH

Bring threaded needle out from back to front at lower left edge of the knitted stitch (or stitches) to be covered. Working from left to right, *insert needle at the upper right edges of the same stitch(es) and bring it back out at the lower left edge of the adjacent stitch, directly below and in line with the insertion point. Work from right to left to work the other half of the cross.

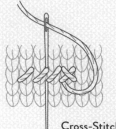

Cross-Stitch

DUPLICATE STITCH

Bring threaded needle out from back to front at the base of the V of the knitted stitch you want to cover. *Working right to left, pass needle in and out under the stitch in the row above it and back into the base of the same stitch. Bring needle back out at the base of the V of the next stitch to the left. Repeat from * for desired number of stitches.

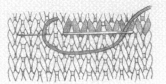

Duplicate Stitch

FRENCH KNOT

Bring threaded needle out of knitted background from back to front, wrap yarn around needle three times, and use your thumb to hold the wraps in place while you insert the needle into the background a short distance from where it came out. Pull the needle through the wraps into the background.

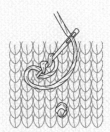

French Knot

STEM STITCH

Bring threaded needle out of knitted background from back to front at the center of a knitted stitch. *Insert the needle into the upper right edge of the next stitch to the right, then out again at the center of the stitch below. Repeat from * as desired.

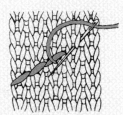

Stem Stitch

STRAIGHT STITCH

Bring threaded needle in and out of background to form a dashed line.

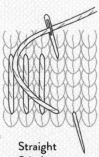

Straight Stitch

Abbreviations

beg	beginning; begin; begins	**M1**	make one (increase)	**sl st**	slip stitch (sl 1 st pwise unless otherwise indicated)
bet	between	**M1R (L)**	make one right (left)	**ssk**	slip 1 kwise, slip 1 kwise, k2 sl sts tog tbl (decrease)
BO	bind off	**p**	purl		
CC	contrasting color	**p1f&b**	purl into front and back of same st	**ssp**	slip 1 kwise, slip 1 kwise, p2 sl sts tog tbl (decrease)
cm	centimeter(s)	**p2tog**	purl two stitches together	**st(s)**	stitch(es)
cn	cable needle	**patt(s)**	pattern(s)	**St st**	stockinette stitch
CO	cast on	**pm**	place marker	**tbl**	through back loop
cont	continue(s); continuing	**psso**	pass slipped stitch over	**tog**	together
dec(s)	decrease(s); decreasing	**p2sso**	pass two slipped stitches over	**WS**	wrong side
dpn	double-pointed needle(s)	**pwise**	purlwise	**wyb**	with yarn in back
foll	following; follows	**RC**	right cross	**wyf**	with yarn in front
g	gram(s)	**rem**	remain(s); remaining	**yo**	yarn over
inc	increase(s); increasing	**rep**	repeat; repeating	*****	repeat starting point (i.e., repeat from *)
k	knit	**rev St st**	reverse stockinette stitch		
k1f&b	knit into front and back of same st	**rib**	ribbing	*** ***	repeat all instructions between asterisks
k2tog	knit two stitches together	**rnd(s)**	round(s)	**( )**	alternate measurements and/or instructions
kwise	knitwise	**RS**	right side		
LC	left cross	**rev sc**	reverse single crochet	**[ ]**	instructions that are to be worked as a group a specified number of times
m(s)	marker(s)	**sc**	single crochet		
MC	main color	**sk**	skip		
mm	millimeter(s)	**sl**	slip		

Glossary

Bind-Offs

Sewn Bind-Off

Cut yarn three times the width of the knitting to be bound off and thread onto a tapestry needle. Working from right to left, *insert tapestry needle purlwise (from right to left) through the first two stitches (**Figure 1**) and pull the yarn through. Bring tapestry needle knitwise (from left to right) through first stitch (**Figure 2**), pull yarn through, and slip this stitch off the knitting needle. Repeat from * for desired number of stitches.

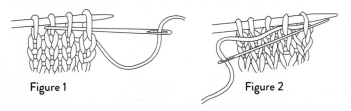

Figure 1   Figure 2

Standard Bind-Off

Knit the first stitch, *knit the next stitch (two stitches on right needle), insert left needle tip into first stitch on right needle (**Figure 1**) and lift this stitch up and over the second stitch (**Figure 2**) and off the needle (**Figure 3**). Repeat from * for the desired number of stitches.

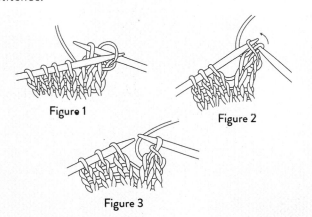

Figure 1   Figure 2

Figure 3

Three-Needle Bind-Off

Place the stitches to be joined onto two separate needles and hold the needles parallel so that the right sides of knitting face together. Insert a third needle into the first stitch on each of two needles (**Figure 1**) and knit them together as one stitch (**Figure 2**), *knit the next stitch on each needle the same way, then use the left needle tip to lift the first stitch over the second and off the needle (**Figure 3**). Repeat from * until no stitches remain on first two needles. Cut yarn and pull tail through last stitch to secure.

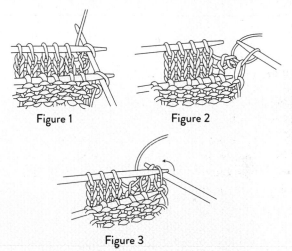

Figure 1   Figure 2

Figure 3

Tubular Bind-Off

Cut the yarn, leaving a tail about 3 times the circumference of the knitting to be bound off, and thread the tail onto a tapestry needle.

STEP 1: Working from right to left, insert the tapestry needle purlwise (from right to left) through the first (knit) stitch (**Figure 1**) and pull the yarn through.

STEP 2: Bring the tapestry needle behind the knit stitch, then insert it knitwise (from left to right) into the second stitch (this will be a purl stitch; **Figure 2**), and pull the yarn through.

STEP 3: *Insert the tapestry needle into the first knit stitch knitwise and slip this stitch off the knitting needle.

STEP 4: Skip the first purl stitch, insert the tapestry needle purlwise into the next knit stitch (**Figure 3**), and pull the yarn through.

STEP 5: Insert the tapestry needle into the first purl stitch purlwise and slip this stitch off the knitting needle.

STEP 6: Bring the tapestry needle behind the knit stitch, then insert it knitwise into the second stitch (this will be a purl stitch; **Figure 4**), and pull the yarn through.

Repeat from * until 1 stitch remains on the knitting needle. Insert the tapestry needle purlwise through this last stitch, draw the yarn through, and pull tight to secure.

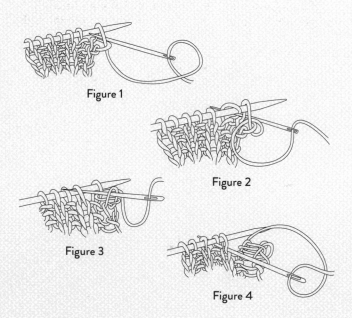

Figure 1

Figure 2

Figure 3

Figure 4

Cast-Ons
Backward-Loop Cast-On

*Loop working yarn and place it on needle backward so that it doesn't unwind. Repeat from *.

Cable Cast-On

If there are no stitches on the needles, make a slipknot of working yarn and place it on the needle, then use the knitted method to cast on one more stitch—two stitches on needle. Hold needle with working yarn in your left hand. *Insert right needle between the first two stitches on left needle (**Figure 1**), wrap yarn around needle as if to knit, draw yarn through (**Figure 2**), and place new loop on left needle (**Figure 3**) to form a new stitch. Repeat from * for the desired number of stitches, always working between the first two stitches on the left needle.

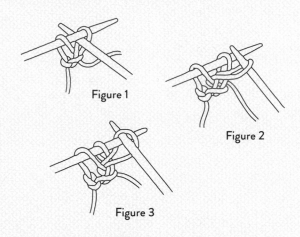

Figure 1

Figure 2

Figure 3

Crochet Chain Provisional Cast-On

With waste yarn and crochet hook, make a loose crochet chain (see above) about four stitches more than you need to cast on. With knitting needle, working yarn, and beginning two stitches from end of chain, pick up and knit one stitch through the back loop of each crochet chain (**Figure 1**) for desired number of stitches. When you're ready to work in the opposite direction, place the exposed loops on a knitting needle as you pull out the crochet chain (**Figure 2**).

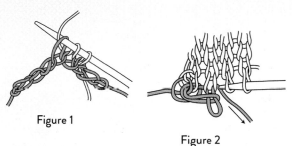

Figure 1

Figure 2

Knitted Cast-On

Place slipknot on left needle if there are no established stitches. *With right needle, knit into first stitch (or slipknot) on left needle (**Figure 1**) and place new stitch onto left needle (**Figure 2**). Repeat from *, always knitting into last stitch made.

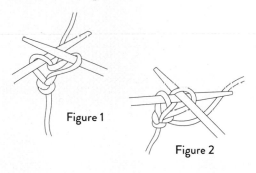

Figure 1

Figure 2

Tubular Cast-On

With contrasting waste yarn, use the backward-loop method to cast on half the desired number of stitches, rounding to the next odd number if necessary (the number can be adjusted after working the cast-on). Cut waste yarn. Continue with working yarn as follows:

ROW 1: K1, *bring yarn to front to form a yarnover, k1 (**Figure 1**); repeat from * to end of row.

ROWS 2 AND 4: K1, *bring yarn to front, slip 1 pwise, bring yarn to back, k1 (**Figure 2**); repeat from * to end of row.

ROWS 3 AND 5: Bring yarn to front, *slip 1 pwise, bring yarn to back, k1, bring yarn to front; repeat from * to last stitch, slip last stitch.

Continue working k1, p1 rib as desired, removing waste yarn after a few rows.

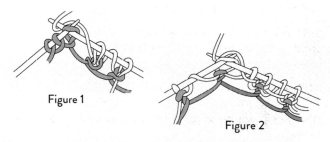

Figure 1

Figure 2

Crochet
Crochet Chain (ch)

Make a slipknot on hook. Yarn over hook and draw it through loop of slipknot. Repeat, drawing yarn through the last loop formed.

Decreases

Knit 2 Together (k2tog)

Knit two stitches together as if they were a single stitch.

Knit 2 Together Through Back Loops (k2tog tbl)

Knit two stitches together through their back loops.

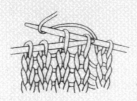

Purl 2 Together (p2tog)

Purl 2 stitches together as if they were a single stitch.

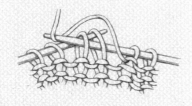

Purl 2 Together Through Back Loops (p2tog tbl)

Bring right needle tip behind two stitches on left needle, enter through the back loop of the second stitch, then the first stitch, then purl them together.

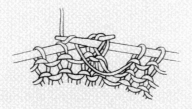

Slip, Slip, Knit (ssk)

Slip two stitches knitwise one at a time (**Figure 1**). Insert point of left needle into front of two slipped stitches and knit them together through back loops with right needle (**Figure 2**).

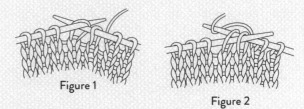

Figure 1   Figure 2

Grafting

Kitchener Stitch (St st Grafting)

STEP 1: Bring threaded needle through front stitch as if to purl and leave stitch on needle (**Figure 1**).

STEP 2: Bring threaded needle through back stitch as if to knit and leave stitch on needle (**Figure 2**).

STEP 3: Bring threaded needle through first front stitch as if to knit and slip this stitch off needle. Bring threaded needle through next front stitch as if to purl and leave stitch on needle (**Figure 3**).

STEP 4: Bring threaded needle through first back stitch as if to purl (as illustrated), slip this stitch off, bring needle through next back stitch as if to knit, leave this stitch on needle (**Figure 4**).

Repeat Steps 3 and 4 until no stitches remain on needles.

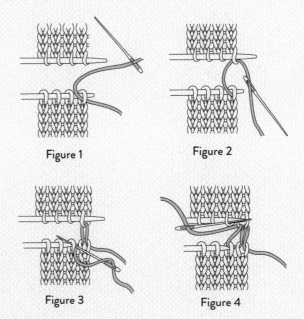

Figure 1   Figure 2

Figure 3   Figure 4

Increases

Bar Increase Knitwise (k1f&b)

Knit into a stitch but leave it on the left needle (**Figure 1**), then knit through the back loop of the same stitch (**Figure 2**) and slip the original stitch off the needle (**Figure 3**).

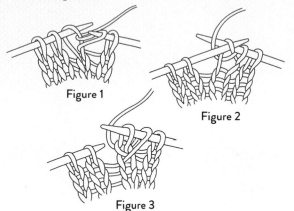

Figure 1

Figure 2

Figure 3

Raised (M1) Increases

Left Slant (M1L) and Standard M1

With left needle tip, lift strand between needles from front to back (**Figure 1**). Knit lifted loop through the back (**Figure 2**).

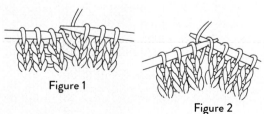

Figure 1

Figure 2

Right Slant (M1R)

With left needle tip, lift strand between needles from back to front (**Figure 1**). Knit lifted loop through the front (**Figure 2**).

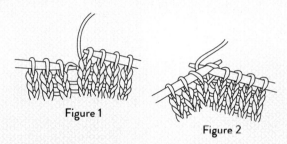

Figure 1

Figure 2

Purl (M1P)

For purl versions, work as above, purling lifted loop.

Pick Up and Knit

Pick Up and Knit along CO or BO Edge

With right side facing and working from right to left, insert the tip of the needle into the center of the stitch below the bind-off or cast-on edge (**Figure 1**), wrap yarn around needle, and pull through a loop (**Figure 2**). Pick up one stitch for every existing stitch.

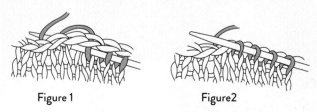

Figure 1

Figure2

Seams

Mattress Stitch Seam

With RS of knitting facing, use threaded needle to pick up one bar between first two stitches on one piece (**Figure 1**), then corresponding bar plus the bar above it on other piece (**Figure 2**). *Pick up next two bars on first piece, then next two bars on other (**Figure 3**). Repeat from * to end of seam, finishing by picking up last bar (or pair of bars) at the top of first piece.

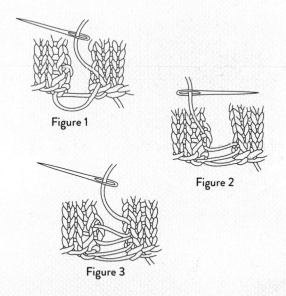

Figure 1

Figure 2

Figure 3

Short-Rows
Knit Side

Work to turn point, slip next stitch purlwise to right needle. Bring yarn to front (**Figure 1**). Slip same stitch back to left needle (**Figure 2**). Turn work and bring yarn in position for next stitch, wrapping the slipped stitch as you do so.

note: *Hide wraps on a knit stitch when right side of piece is worked as a knit stitch. Leave wrap if the purl stitch shows on the right side.*

Hide wraps as follows: Knit stitch: On right side, work to just before wrapped stitch, insert right needle from front, under the wrap from bottom up, and then into wrapped stitch as usual. Knit them together, making sure the new stitch comes out under the wrap. Purl stitch: On wrong side, work to just before wrapped stitch. Insert right needle from back, under wrap from bottom up, and put on left needle. Purl lifted wrap and stitch together.

Purl Side

Work to the turning point, slip the next stitch purlwise to the right needle, bring the yarn to the back of the work (**Figure 1**), return the slipped stitch to the left needle, bring the yarn to the front between the needles (**Figure 2**), and turn the work so that the knit side is facing—one stitch has been wrapped and the yarn is correctly positioned to knit the next stitch. To hide the wrap on a subsequent purl row, work to the wrapped stitch, use the tip of the right needle to pick up the wrap from the back, place it on the left needle (**Figure 3**), then purl it together with the wrapped stitch.

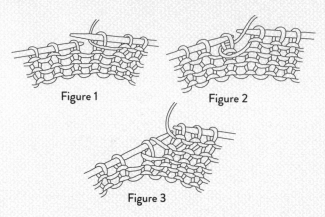

Figure 1   Figure 2

Figure 3

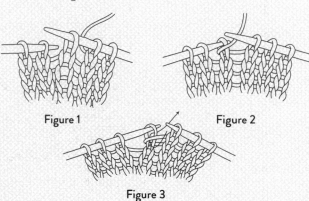

Figure 1   Figure 2

Figure 3

Sources for Yarns

Berroco
1 Tupperware Dr., Ste. 4
North Smithfield, RI 02896
(401) 769-1212
berroco.com

Bijou Basin Ranch
bijoubasinranch.com

Blackberry Ridge
3776 Forshaug Rd.
Mount Horeb, WI 53572
(608) 437-3762
blackberry-ridge.com

Brooklyn Tweed
brooklyntweed.net

Classic Elite Yarns
16 Esquire Rd., Unit 2
North Billerica, MA 01862
(800) 343-0308
classiceliteyarns.com

Dale of Norway
4750 Shelburne Rd., Ste. 20
Shelburne, VT 05482
dalegarn.no

Jaggerspun
jaggeryarn.com

Lorna's Laces
4229 N. Honore St.
Chicago, IL 60613
(773) 935-3803
lornaslaces.net

Louet North America
3425 Hands Rd.
Prescott, ON
Canada K0E 1T0
(800) 897-6444
louet.com

Malabrigo
(786) 866-6187
malabrigoyarn.com

Mirasol
mirasol.com.pe

Plymouth
500 Lafayette St.
Bristol, PA 19007
(215) 788-0459
plymouthyarn.com

Quince & Company
quinceandco.com

Rowan
Green Lane Mill
Holmfirth, West Yorkshire
England HD9 2DX
44 (0)1484 681881
knitrowan.com

USA:
Westminster Fibers
165 Ledge St.
Nashua, NH 03060
(800) 445-9276
westminsterfibers.com

Sundara Yarn
sundarayarn.com

Tahki Stacy Charles
70-60 83rd St., Bldg. #12
Glendale, NY 11385
(718) 326-4433
tahkistacycharles.com

The Fibre Company
2000 Manor Rd.
Conshohocken, PA 19428
thefibreco.com

Trendsetter Yarns
16745 Saticoy St. #101
Van Nuys, CA 91406
(800) 446-2425
trendsetteryarns.com

Ullcentrum Öland
Byrumsvägen 59
387 74 Löttorp
Sweden
46 (0) 485 29010
ullcentrum.com

Index

If you love knitted accessories,

you'll love these inspirational resources from Interweave

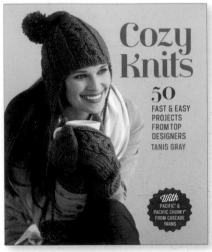

Join Knittingdaily.com, an online community that
shares your passion for knitting. You'll get a free
eNewsletter, free patterns, projects store, a daily blog,
event updates, galleries, tips and techniques, and
more. Sign up for *Knitting Daily* at **Knittingdaily.com.**

KNITS

INTERWEAVE

From cover to cover, *Interweave Knits* magazine
presents great projects for the beginner to the
advanced knitter. Every issue is packed full of
captivating smart designs, step-by-step instructions,
easy-to-understand illustrations, plus well-written,
lively articles sure to inspire. **Interweaveknits.com**